Catfishes

The complete guide to the successful care and breeding of more than 100 catfish species

Lee Finley

Catfishes

Project Team
Editor: David E. Boruchowitz
Indexer: Elizabeth Walker
Design: Mary Ann Kahn

T.F.H. Publications
President/CEO: Glen S. Axelrod
Executive Vice President: Mark E. Johnson
Publisher: Christopher T. Reggio
Production Manager: Kathy Bontz

T.F.H. Publications, Inc.
One TFH Plaza
Third and Union Avenues
Neptune City, NJ 07753

Printed and bound in China
09 10 11 12 13 1 3 5 7 9 8 6 4 2

Library of Congress Cataloging-in-Publication Data
Finley, Lee.
  Catfishes : the complete guide to the successful care and breeding of more than 100 catfish species / Lee Finley.
     p. cm.
  Includes index.
  ISBN 978-0-7938-1677-4 (alk. paper)
  1. Catfishes. I. Title.
  SF458.C38F56 2009
  639.3'7492--dc22
                         2009017510

The Leader In Responsible Animal Care For Over 50 Years!®
www.tfh.com

CENTRAL
Garden & Pet

Contents

Introduction

I would like to say a few words about aquarium catfishes. Well, okay, it will take more than a few words. In fact, I could use many more words than my allotted allowance for this project. But within the framework that I have been kindly provided I will give it my best attempt.

There are so many catfishes on the planet! They can be found on every continent except Antarctica. Currently there are almost 3,200 described species. The number of undescribed species, although only partially known, will no doubt add significantly to this number. To give an idea of the catfishes' place in the overall scheme of fishes,

consider the following. Approximately 25 percent of all freshwater fish species, 10 percent of all fish species, and 5 percent of all vertebrate species are catfish. With this in mind, trying to offer an overview of all catfishes in this space is a daunting

task. There are catfish books much larger than this one that predominately cover only one genus and maybe about 200 species. So obviously a different approach is needed: looking at catfish as potential aquarium specimens.

The first few chapters of this book are aimed at providing some general information on catfishes and their place as aquarium inhabitants. This includes thoughts on the choosing of catfishes, their initial care, foods and feeding, and some aspects of breeding them. Also included is a look at catfish spines and the potential problems these can cause. The last chapter of this book offers a look at some of the various catfish families and some of the species contained within them. Hopefully this section will help to lay a base for an overall appreciation of the catfishes and their great diversity.

I hope that this book will increase your interest in catfishes and prod you to go searching for more information. There are numerous in-print and out-of-print books on aquarium catfishes. Seek these out. Periodical publications are also a good source of continually published material. Subscribe to these. And then there is the Internet with its overall anything-goes approach. But even with this it's the place where information shows up first and regularly. Find the good websites, stay with them, and support them. Start with Planet Catfish and ScotCat. The catfish world expands from there.

Choosing Catfishes

The variety found among catfishes is nothing short of amazing. While on any given visit to your local aquarium store you might see a reasonable selection that most likely will be heavy on South American *Corydoras* and loricariid (plecos) species, over time you'll begin to grasp the great amount of other catfishes that exists. Many species are seasonal in their hobby appearance, and new species (or old ones that haven't been imported for some time) are constantly becoming more available. When the whole picture is put together, you'll see what makes this group so desirable and attractive to so many aquarists.

C. paleatus, usually sold as the peppered cory, is a commonly available cory cat. It is one of the easiest species to keep and breed.

As you work your visual way through the catfishes available to you, it's good to try to learn as you go. You obviously won't be purchasing all of the catfishes that you see, but you should take mental notes on at least some of those species and try to research them. This will set the stage and make you better prepared should you at some time see a particular species again and say, "I'm going to take some of those (or that one) home."

With many groups of catfishes you can deal more or less in generalities. A great many of the *Corydoras* species, a South American group, will fall into this niche. But generalities may not always be successful, and you will have to make, for example, some differentiation between the more standard *Corydoras* species (*C. aeneus*, *C. delphax*, *C. paleatus*, etc.), and the genus's smaller mid-water swimmers, such as *C. pygmaeus* and *C. hastatus*. Likewise, generalities apply also to the popular *Synodontis* species. As a group these African catfishes adapt exceedingly well to aquarium life, but you must make decisions in regard to the size range that you would like to maintain—4 inches (10 cm) or 1 foot (30 cm)—and the behavioral characteristics that you are looking for. Do you want a model catfish for a peaceful tank or a species that's tough enough to hold its own with a batch of rowdy tankmates? If you're at least partially armed with such information, you're already on the way towards success with a chosen fish. Of course, not every catfish can be easily known or figured out, but as long as you do your best conferring with various literature sources (paper and electronic), other aquarists, and store personnel, you have embarked on the proper path.

Three Important Traits to Consider

As I've already mentioned, there are three major areas in the pursuit of catfish knowledge that are very important in your preparatory stages. Of course, there are numerous other aspects as well, and many of those aspects will be looked at as we move along.

Wh
to

When resear
interest you, l
on their beh
sizes; look al
about poten
recommendations aic ...
topics can help you decide whether the catfishes would do well in a small community tank, a tank devoted to large fishes, or a single-specimen tank.

Behavior

The first area is that of behavior. If you have a tank of peaceful fishes and wish to add an interesting catfish or two, the last thing that you want is to add a species that's going to upset the pastoral pleasantness that you're enjoying. As an example, there are two *Synodontis* catfishes that are at least superficially similar in appearance—*S. congica* and *S. notata*. Both have a silvery to grayish body coloration and are adorned with varying numbers of round black spots on their sides. *S. congica* would be a model catfish for such a peaceful tank. *S. notata*, although not a terribly destructive catfish, can be more than a bit boisterous, especially as it grows. *S. congica* is pretty much always going to be peaceful. The same cannot be said with certainty about *S. notata*.

Predation

Trying to figure out who might eat who also needs consideration. This might sound a little flip, but it's truly a serious consideration. Many catfishes eat other fishes, and their capacities in this regard can be downright amazing at times. Many years ago, when I was predominately a cichlid keeper, I had a couple of tanks of various catfishes. On one shopping trip I returned home with a cute pseudopimelodid, *Batrochoglanis raninus*, that was about 3½ inches (9 cm) long. I knew that this large-mouthed species had a reputation for eating smaller fishes, so I chose its tankmates carefully. The smallest fish in the tank was a nice South American whiptail cat, *Rineloricaria* sp., that was about 5½

Synodontis notata may be too active and rambunctious for many hobbyists, but other *Synodontis* species are more peaceful.

inches (14 cm) long. No problem, right? Wrong! The following morning I went down to the fishroom and was greeted with an amazing sight. Protruding from the new fish's mouth was about 3 inches (8 cm) of the rear end of the whiptail cat! Over the next few days the whiptail disappeared into the pseudopimelodid. I wasn't amused, but I did learn an important lesson—never underestimate what a predatory catfish might be able to swallow.

Size

Lastly I must say a word about the potential size of catfishes intended to be kept in home aquaria. Some simply don't belong in home aquaria; they get too big or too nasty or both. This is my personal opinion, and I do feel some discussion on this is necessary.

As might be expected of a group of fishes containing over 3,000 species, there are some very large catfishes. Large is, of course, a subjective word, and I take it herein to mean in relation to the size of the containers (aquaria) that we keep our fishes in. To set the stage for the following I will note that the catfish group of fishes also contains an amazing number of species that are small to medium-sized (say 1 foot [30 cm] or less) and are therefore more or less ideal to acceptable inhabitants for the home aquarium. (A lot depends on the size of your aquarium, obviously—many aquarists would consider a foot-long fish to be a good deal bigger than "medium-sized.") There are quite a few that get a bit larger than this but, based on their mild deportment and habits, can still be considered for keeping in big tanks if that's your cup of tea.

If there's a poster cat for large catfishes not belonging in aquaria it's surely the South American redtail catfish, *Phractocephalus hemioliopterus*. At a small size (2 to 3 inches [5 to 8 cm]) this colorful pimelodid is almost irresistible. It pretty much has everything going for it: color, interesting appearance, and personality. But things can turn sour when you realize that this catfish eventually reaches a total length of almost 4½ feet (1.4 m)! If anything else is needed to cap this, a healthy redtail of this size weighs in at about 100 pounds (45 kg).

What is the home aquarist to do with a fully grown redtail, or even one that attains between half and three-quarters of the maximum size, which is still an enormous fish? The potential problem is actually twofold. The first scenario is maybe the worse of the two. This is where an unknowing, and often newer, aquarist purchases a small redtail without knowing its size potential. Or, worse, even knowing it goes ahead with the purchase. This will eventually lead to an unhappy catfish and an owner of equal sentiment. Sometimes a store might take the fish back, but this isn't a certainty. What then? Will the fish languish and eventually die in cramped and environmentally poor conditions? Will it be euthanized? Will it be released into local waters? None of these outcomes is acceptable and/or fair to such a potentially magnificent catfish.

Certainly at least some dedicated aquarists like to keep large fishes. While such aquarists have large tanks for their charges, it's impossible in a realistic sense to provide a big enough tank for an adult redtail catfish unless something akin to a public-style aquarium is built in one's home. Extremely rare are even the most dedicated of aquarists who might be willing to go this necessary extra mile.

I could list many other catfishes and note the potential sizes that they might reach, but hopefully by now you've gotten the point. If you're new to catfishes, research your

Although it is beautiful and commonly available, the redtail catfish grows too large for all but the most dedicated hobbyists and the biggest tanks.

The journey made by most wild-caught catfishes to your home tank is often a long one: from the collector of the fish in its native waters to the exporter, then from the importer to the wholesaler and then to your local store and then lastly to your tank. Breeding of catfishes by commercial breeders and local hobbyists forms an important exception to this pathway. Although there is an increasing variety available, most domestically bred catfishes will consist of some loricariids (e.g., *Ancistrus* spp.) and various *Corydoras*. Another group often available is some of the Lake Tanganyikan *Synodontis* species, such as *S. lucipinnis* and *S. multipunctata*.

Most catfishes offered for sale come from the wild, from fish farms in Florida or Southeast Asia, and from breeders in eastern Europe. Some of the fishes from this last-named source, however, are hybrids (see the *Synodontis* section in Chapter 5).

purchases and make sure that you're ready to proceed. If you're a large-fishes aquarist, start saving up for that new large tank!

Making Your Decision

The potential last step of the buying process is to purchase or not to purchase any of the catfishes that you see. Although the store workers can assist you in such decisions, in the end you're the final arbiter. Aquarium stores don't want to sell you sick fishes, as this will not be good for their business in the long run. But, again, you have the final say with your purchases, and extra vigilance regarding them will benefit you greatly.

Pick from a Healthy Tank

First, you want to look around a store tank and make sure that it has healthy-looking fishes. If one fish, of any kind, has what might be a spreadable condition or disease, move on. This isn't a tank that you want to choose fish from. Most stores will recognize such problems and quarantine the tank, but you should do your own overview just to be sure.

You should give any potential purchase a good visual going over. With this you should carefully consider both the positive and negative aspects of the particular catfish. This should include a basic health check regarding the physical condition and close observation of the behavior exhibited by the fish. With many catfishes this might present some initial problems in that they may very well, after their travel, be more of a mind to hide away among the tank's decor than to present themselves to you for inspection. Here is where store personnel can be helpful by gently going into the tank with a net or other object and making sure that you can get a good look at your potential purchase.

Physical Appearance

For general physical conditions, you will want to make sure that the catfish has no bloody areas on the body or the fins (especially at the edges). Also look for any fuzzy patches that might indicate a wound that will lead to a subsequent fungal infection.

Carefully inspect any catfish before you buy it, paying special attention to its barbels.

Such funguses often appear at the ends of the dorsal or pectoral spines of many catfishes. They aren't an immediate threat, but if you do purchase such a catfish you will then be responsible for taking the appropriate actions to treat the infection. You will also want to look closely at the body to make sure that there is no thin grayish/whitish coating, which might be indicative of an external bacterial infection. The eyes are a good place to check extra close for this. Many catfishes will show a deep reflective appearance, but this is normal. Some catfishes, such as talking cats (doradids), may normally show a whitish cast to the eyes and body (especially the head area), but with some experience you can easily differentiate this condition from a potential bacterial infection.

Parasitic infections also need to be considered. Ich, also called white spot disease, is one to watch for, especially during cool-to-cold times of the year. In one stage of its life cycle the parasite shows as small scattered white spots on the body and fins of an infected fish. Some driftwood catfishes (auchenipterids), such as *Auchenipterichthys coracoideus,* show a definite pattern of small white spots on their bodies. While these spots may superficially resemble ich, the regularity of the pattern—as opposed to the randomness of ich—is the tip-off that the spots are normal.

The barbels are another area to check out. Try to make sure that they are not shortened, bloody, or missing. You can compare the barbels of a fish you're interested in against those of an ideal specimen if you're familiar with the species, or you can compare the fish with others of the same species in the tank.

The Catfish–Barbel Connection

Catfishes are famous for their barbels. In fact, the order Siluriformes, to which all of the catfishes belong, got its common name from the fishes' barbels. They almost look like a cat's whiskers. Other freshwater fishes, including carps, arowanas, and loaches, also have barbels, but usually the first fish that comes to mind when a hobbyist hears the word "barbel" or "whiskers" is a catfish.

Catfish barbels vary in length from species to species. Cory cats have small barbels to match their small size, while others, such as Sorubim lima and Pimelodus spp., have barbels that are several inches long.

Thinness: Many catfishes, especially those that have recently arrived at a store, may often be quite thin. This is common, as feeding is often quite light along the various stages of transit. Thinness is normal, but there are extremes to the situation that are best avoided. This situation is especially notable with various loricariids. Because these catfishes usually stay close to the substrate it can often be difficult to get a good look at their abdominal areas. It's a good idea to get a store worker to net a potential purchase from among these fishes so that you can get a good look at the fish's underside. Some thinness is acceptable, but if the stomach area is heavily caved in you might want to consider coming back later, after the fish is settled in and eating, before making a purchase. Another area to check on loricariids is the eyes. Beware if the eyes are sunken into the head, below the rim of the eye socket. This is often a sign of severe starvation, usually coupled with a noticeably caved-in abdominal area. While loricariids in this condition might be brought back into good health with proper feeding, this cannot be considered a sure thing, and generally speaking such a catfish should be avoided. There are some loricariids, such as the royal pleco, *Panaque nigrolineatus*, that can actually pull their eyes down into the socket, but this is a form of protection, and the eyes don't stay sunken for very long. If you see such a royal pleco in which the eyes are sunken, and remain so, you will be better off avoiding it and waiting for another one.

Behavior In the Seller's Tank

How catfishes are behaving is another important consideration. Observe their breathing to make sure that it's normal. A steady respiration can be judged by observing the movements of the mouth and their gill covers. A rapid respiration observed on a resting catfish can often be a sign of a bacterial or parasitic infection on the gills or some other form of physical stress.

Also observe how a fish holds itself in the water. Here you do need to know something regarding the behavior of a particular species or group of species. For example, take some of the standard *Corydoras* species such as *C. aeneus, C. paleatus,* and many of the spotted forms that may collectively be sold as *C. punctatus*. These are primarily bottom-based catfishes, and if you see them hanging in mid-water or at the surface, you can be assured that there's a problem of some sort. It could be poor water conditions in the tank, but it could also indicate some type of organic problem. In either case, these sick fish shouldn't be brought home. These *Corydoras* should be actively moving around the lower part of the tank, with the occasional dash to the surface to grab a bubble of air (which they swallow and extract oxygen from in their gut). On the other hand, there are some *Corydoras* species that spend more time away from the bottom. Members of the *C. elegans* complex (*C. elegans, C. napoensis,* etc.) often fit into this group. And some of the smaller cories, such as *C. pygmaeus* and *C. hastatus,* are normally mid-water swimmers. If these diminutive species are lying on the bottom, or are swimming around near the surface in a dopey fashion, it's not a good sign, and they should be avoided.

Additional Sources of Catfishes

One additional area that needs to be touched on is the purchase of catfishes that you can't see in advance. Previously this type of business was generally done by mail or via the telephone, but the Internet and e-mail are now more typically the methods used for communication. There is nothing wrong with purchasing catfishes in this way. Many of the specialty dealers will often have a much wider variety of hard-to-find catfishes in stock than you might usually find at your local stores. But this availability does come with the fact that you can't see the catfishes beyond a digital photo or possibly a short video. In cases of purchasing catfishes by this method it's better to use the phone and talk with the party or parties involved. A short phone call can

The royal pleco can pull its eyes down into their sockets for protection, but avoid any individual with eyes that stay sunken.

You must also take the cost of delivery from online retailers into consideration. While prices of catfishes at such a specialty dealer may be less than those at your local sources, you must factor in the cost of the fast delivery that's needed to get the catfishes to you. This will often add substantially to the total cost. But if in this way you're able to obtain desired catfishes that are unavailable in your area, it can be considered worth it.

provide good information on the potential purchase much better than an e-mail can. That is my opinion and I'll stand by it. A phone call is also much better for developing a relationship with such a provider.

A more recent method of obtaining catfishes also comes to us via the Internet—the purchase of catfishes by auction. While some aquarium fishes have been seen for some time on larger Internet auction sites, the specialty sites are a bit newer, and some of them serve as a platform for the auctioning of an amazing amount of fishes—catfishes included. I haven't personally obtained any catfishes by this method, so I cannot offer specific comments beyond, as mentioned earlier, working on developing a good rapport with the source.

Going Home

I'm returning you now to your local store and your recent purchase. Your store will bag your fishes, and many stores will use a double-bag method for most catfishes. This is good practice, but for certain species, such as the larger *Synodontis*, it is rarely sufficient. Such catfishes, with their large pectoral fin spines, will often need three or more bags. And even with this, a quick movement by the fish will easily send a pectoral spine right through the multiple bags. For moving such catfishes I would suggest using a plastic bucket with a cover. It's always good to have some of these buckets handy. Most stores have them and will probably be happy to lend you one if necessary. Another way of moving larger catfishes is with a large shipping bag (stores will also have these on hand) inside a rigid foam shipping box. Catfishes are moved all over the world like this—why not to your home from the store?

During those times of the year when it's too cold or too hot, it's best to have an insulated container into which you can put your bagged catfish. Rigid foam fish shipping boxes, often enclosed within a cardboard box, are ideal for this purpose; usually your store can supply you with one for a minimal charge. Likewise, you can also carry a picnic-style cooler along with you on shopping expeditions. This little bit of extra protection is well worth having.

Welcome Home

Once home, the next thing to do is to get your catfishes into their tank—or is it?

As you build up a nice collection of catfishes, or other fishes for that matter, the protection of these animals is your responsibility. Every aquarist finds out sooner or later that the introduction of a new fish into an established aquarium, no matter how healthy they appear, may bring in a disease that spreads and affects the previously healthy inhabitants. This can range from a minor annoyance to a major disaster. One way of avoiding such a situation is through the use of a quarantine tank (or tanks). It takes more effort to maintain a quarantine setup, but in the long run it will help to prevent some problems that you would prefer not have to deal with.

Quarantine

Many aquarists regularly put all newly acquired fishes through a quarantine period. Obviously you need to be able to set up a separate tank for the quarantine process, and the situation might require a little more thought and planning than just dumping a new acquistion into an already occupied aquarium, but it will in the long run be well worth it.

Water: In setting up such a tank I generally use half new water and half water from the tank that the catfish will eventually call home. In regard to the latter water, I would suggest doing a 15- to 20-percent water change on the tank first before its water is

Many catfish, including *Synodontis ocellifer*, have spiny fins, so it is a good idea to transport them in a covered bucket rather than a plastic bag.

Depending on the size of the new catfish(es) involved, a suitable quarantine tank can usually range from 5 to 20 gallons (20 to 80 liters). As the water chemistry in larger tanks tends to be more stable, it would be wise to gravitate towards them. The basics of a quarantine setup will include:

• the tank
• a submersible heater of proper wattage (unless you have a heated fishroom)
• a filter (an air-driven box filter of medium size or a small to medium-sized overflow-type power filter)
• a cover for the tank
• a couple of hiding places for the inhabitants

You can use a small strip light if you wish, but this isn't really necessary. I usually don't use gravel in a quarantine tank, but a thin layer can be added if you so desire.

added to the quarantine tank. The fish in both tanks will enjoy the new water, because it will be of a fresher quality. Treat the new water as needed for chlorine, chloramine, etc.

Temperature and Filtration: You should get the heater going and adjust the water temperature. From here you can set up your filter. You will want to have biological filtration—this is fairly easy to get going. You can take a medium-sized (or larger) box filter and fill it half to three-quarters full with gravel from a healthy, functioning tank. Place some filter fiber material over the gravel and hook the filter to an air source. You now have a functional filter with a biologically active component. You may also use some pieces of an active sponge filter in the box filter if you wish. Just use some filter floss over them to protect them against quickly clogging. An active sponge filter can also be used alone. Some aquarists prefer the sponge filter, but I prefer the additional particle removal provided by the box filter. If you wish to use carbon or some other medium in the box filter you can do so easily by putting it into a small nylon bag and placing it on the gravel before adding the floss. Just remember that if you decide to use medications to treat an illness the carbon will need to be removed from the filter.

Acclimation: You should have the quarantine tank all set up before you get your new fish home; then you can immediately acclimate the newcomer(s). Handle this as you would with introducing the fish to a regular tank: Slowly add water from the tank to the bag until the volume has been doubled. From here you can net the catfish (using a tight-weave net) and release it into the tank. Dispose of all of the bag water down a drain. I never add any fish store water into my tanks. Fish stores go through a lot of fish, increasing the chance that something unpleasant might sneak in with the water. Call me a little paranoid, but disposing of the water makes me feel better. Additionally, the process of packing the fish and the resultant stress that it undergoes in the bag will lead to the release of various products of metabolism that are best disposed of.

Hiding Places: Hiding places should be in place when the catfish is added to the quarantine tank. Of course, not all catfishes will necessarily use these hiding places, but they should be there just in case. The hiding places should provide good cover and be easily accessible to the catfish. I usually use either PVC pipe of a suitable internal diameter or some of the commercial ceramic bottomless caves that are available at aquarium stores. The main feature that you want here is a hiding (comfort) place for the catfish from which it can easily be removed for observation. Know that catfishes can get into tight places that will make it difficult to easily remove them from for viewing. At least a couple of times a day you should go into the tank and gently move the catfish out of hiding for viewing. A flashlight will be helpful with this. As you did initially in the store, look carefully for any signs of a bacterial or parasitic infection. As noted previously, the fins are an excellent area for observing such conditions.

Quarantine Diet

While your new catfish is in its quarantine quarters you should feed it on a regular basis. A couple of small feedings a day (three or four would be better) should be offered. You can experiment at this stage to find out which foods it prefers. With its austere setup it may be a bit shy, so some evening feeding after all lights are out will be a good idea during this phase.

House newly acquired fish in a quarantine tank to help avoid spreading diseases to your established aquarium.

Length of Quarantine

Usually a week or two of quarantine is sufficient. If the catfish is doing well and hasn't developed any problems, it should be fine to then transfer it to its permanent home. You can move it to a bucket with some of its tank water and then add an equal part of water from the new home tank over a period of time. When this is completed, net the catfish and add it to its new tank. Dispose of the bucket water.

The Catfish Aquarium

Most catfishes will do well in a wide variety of aquarium setups, and these may vary greatly based on the preferences of the individual aquarist. What follows are my personal opinions about catfish tank setups; they are of course open to modification as you might see fit.

Decor

An aquarium is your canvas, and you may decorate it at will. I prefer more natural materials, but depending on the tank inhabitants and the needed purposes I'm very happy using clay pots or drainage pipes, PVC pipes, etc. Generally, most catfishes are more comfortable when they have several readily available hiding places. How you provide them is up to you as long as you avoid potentially dangerous materials.

You can use small clay flowerpots for hiding places in a catfish aquarium.

Lighting

Fluorescent lighting is pretty much the standard for catfish aquaria. A primary consideration, in that there are more types of fluorescent bulbs than you can shake a stick at, is that you need to think out whether you want to maintain living plants in addition to your fishes. Your local store can be of assistance in helping you decide on bulb type should you decide to go with live plants. Although some catfishes are slow to lose their shyness in the presence of brighter light, most will adapt to such conditions and regularly swim around the tank, especially at feeding time.

Substrate

I generally tend to favor natural gravel of small grain size. This is quite standard and is usually sold as No. 3 gravel. It is basically neutral and will not affect water factors such as pH and hardness. However, smaller sizes of substrate, whether gravel or sand, may tend to pack and hold in waste materials, even with proper cleaning. Larger particle sizes also tend to create pockets in which food and waste may get trapped. Lacking the presence of a digging catfish to agitate the gravel somewhat, using too small or too large gravel may create unwanted problems with water quality. With that said, I will note that substrates of small particle size can be good under certain conditions. Some catfishes like to bury themselves in the substrate (*Pseudohemiodon* and *Planiloricaria* spp. come to mind) and ideally sand should be provided as part of their environment—especially if maintaining a single-species tank. The larger-sized gravel can be very attractive, but you should have a larger and more powerful catfish, or a group of them, to help you keep it problem-free. Some of the larger doradids can be excellent for such purposes.

Tank Size

On one level this is simple and based on the size of the given catfish(es) and the minimum amount of room in which they will need to be comfortable. You will need to research your potential purchases and plan accordingly as regards tank size. In that most catfishes will not be kept on an individual basis, an overview of the whole community (mixed or just catfishes) will need to be taken into account. But if you err, always try to do so on the side of caution. For example, a group of some of the small mid-water *Corydoras* (*C. hastatus, C. pygmaeus*) may well be able to get along in a 10-gallon (40-liter) tank, but they will be much better off, and display more natural behavior, in a 20-gallon (80-liter) tank. Oftentimes many catfishes will eventually become too large to be comfortable in the tank that you originally provided for them. When that happens it will be necessary to either get a larger

Recycling Your Water?

The leftover fish store water from the acclimation process, as well as the water from your water changes, doesn't have to be dumped down the drain. If you have indoor plants or an outdoor garden, you can water your plants with it. Dissolved fish wastes do wonders for plant growth.

My Catfish Aquarium Management Philosophy

Catfishes, like practically all other aquarium fishes, are an adaptable bunch. As long as certain conditions are met they will live and thrive in captivity under conditions that they might never encounter in their natural habitats. They can accept a wide variance of pH values, water hardness, and temperatures. There are basic set norms for these conditions, and they work for practically any catfish you care to think of. But there are some things that you need to give them in their aquaria. You need to provide a good, well-considered diet. You need to provide good mechanical and biological filtration, and these systems must be maintained. If they slip, problems will follow. You also need to provide good water quality. The two filtration methods will go a long way towards this, but you must make regular reasonably sized water changes on your fishes' tanks. If you fail to make needed water changes, problems will not be far behind. Sure it requires a bit of work, but your work will produce happy catfishes

tank or trade them in for something smaller. It is always best to use from the start an aquarium large enough for the adult fish.

In General Terms

Again, the previous four topics are in general terms. Species-specific tank sizes, substrates, lighting, and decor will be mentioned as applicable in the various sections of the last chapter.

Catfish Spines and Injuries

Sooner or later you're almost sure to have a run-in with the business end of one or more of your catfish's spines. This can be painful, sometimes frighteningly so, so it's worthy of some discussion.

Aquarium Nets

To begin we must first discuss catfishes and aquarium nets. The strong bony pectoral and dorsal spines that a great many catfishes possess create problems with the standard aquarium nets that are used in the hobby. Such nets tend to have a fairly large mesh size, which allows them to be moved rather quickly through the water.

A tight-weave net with small holes offers strong resistance against the water and makes catching fishes much more difficult. But the more standard larger-weave nets are catfish spine traps in waiting. A catfish's spines can easily push through these larger holes. Making the situation even more problematic is the fact that these spines often have saw-like projections (many times on the front and back of the spines) that easily entangle in the net. And it isn't just one tangle. As the catfish rolls and fights its confinement, multiple openings are gone into and snagged up, and usually several spines can become involved. This whole process can do a substantial amount of damage to the catfish. The soft parts of the fins, with their more delicate supporting rays, get torn, and the superficial layers of the epithelium on the spines are scraped away. The whole unpleasant process opens up these wounded areas to potential subsequent bacterial or fungal attacks. In addition, the overall stress to the catfish caused by this process is bad for its general health. I will note that this description is a worst-case scenario, but a situation like this may happen more often than one would like. Even in a one-spine-in-the-net situation, substantial physical damage and stress can be experienced by the catfish. And it's often during such times as this, while undertaking the difficult task of untangling the catfish, that a spine and the aquarist's hand make unpleasant and painful contact.

Envenomation

Before moving on to some specific examples of potentially problematic catfishes, some general comments regarding the process of envenomation are called for.

A catfish wound is initiated when either the dorsal or one of the pectoral spines breaks your skin. This may be done in the form of a scratch, but usually it's experienced as a puncture wound. In the skin covering on the spines of many catfishes there are varying numbers of special venom-secreting cells. For example, when a spine enters a finger, first there's the physical trauma, followed by the rupture of the secretor cells, which release venom/toxins into the wound. This is a relatively simple

The spiny fins of catfish are prone to getting caught in nets, which can injure the fish.

An Extreme Catfish Spine Injury

Problems regarding the contact of catfish spines with the human anatomy are well recorded in the medical literature. As with any such topic, there are extremes. American ichthyologist Hugh Smith wrote of a case in which a fisherman in Thailand went into the water to help untangle an 8-foot-long (2.4-m-long) *Pangasius sanitwongsei* from a net and suffered a fatal abdominal wound from one of the catfish's pectoral spines. So feel lucky that you wouldn't be keeping something like this in the home aquarium!

and effective form of self defense. To add injury to injury, on occasion pieces of the spine will break off during the event, leaving a foreign body, which will also need to be dealt with.

Some catfishes appear to have another method of envenomation, although there is now some question in regard to this. It has been suggested that they produce venom in an axillary gland located at the base of at least some of the fin spines (generally the pectorals). It has been postulated that during a skin breach by the spine the catfish will release toxin from the gland, and this toxin is then delivered to the wound via grooves in the spine. One catfish in which this might happen is the small *Akysis vespa* (family Akysidae), which is one of the so-called Asian bumblebee catfishes. It's interesting that the species name *vespa* means wasp in Latin. This name was used in a double sense in that the yellow and black color pattern of the fish is like that of many wasps, and maybe more importantly in reference to the fish's extreme stinging ability.

Some Problematic Catfishes

In the medical literature there are reports of catfish stings relating to members of the following families: Ariidae, Auchenipteridae, Bagridae, Clariidae (with probably *Heteropneustes* also involved), Doradidae, Ictaluridae (especially with the smaller North American madtoms, *Noturus* spp.), Pimelodidae (in the wide sense including Pseudopimelodidae and Heptapteridae), Plotosidae, and Siluridae. Based on additional published sources and conversations with many aquarists over the years, it does appear that at least some members of most families of catfishes have the potential to offer up similarly unpleasant experiences—and they don't even need to be alive! A good friend of mine went to pick up a dead *Corydoras* catfish and zigged when he should have zagged; he ended up impaling his finger on a pectoral spine of the deceased catfish. For this he sustained a painful wound that hurt consistently for two days.

Some additional comments need to be made here due to the potential seriousness of getting spined by certain catfishes.

Ariidae: I always tend to argue against the aquarium keeping of members of this family, which are usually sold under common names likening them to sharks. In addition to the other problems with these catfishes, they also fall into the class of being able to deliver a severe wound, especially as they get larger. Fishermen throughout the range of this family are strongly aware of this situation and treat caught fish with great respect.

Heteropneustidae: This is a small Asian family of freshwater catfishes that can be quite dangerous. Because of this they probably don't belong in the hobby. One common name for these catfishes, and not without reason, is stinging catfish. Larger individuals have been implicated in human deaths, but all I have come across are second-hand tellings.

Plotosidae: The freshwater species of this family, which are found in Australia and New Guinea, are noted by ichthyologist Dr. Gerald Allen to be capable of producing extremely painful wounds. There is also a saltwater species that is commonly available to the marine hobby. This species, *Plotosus lineatus,* is commercially known as the coral cat. This is a potentially dangerous species; every caution should be exercised in its presence. The potential for problems is increased because juveniles of this species tend to form schools.

Be Careful

The bottom line is this: be very careful when netting and handling your catfishes. Additionally, be careful when you're working in a tank containing catfishes. The extreme damage from a sting by the fossil cat that I describe in a sidebar on the next page came when the doctor was working in the tank. The catfish spooked and dashed, and before the doctor could even think about removing his hand the damage was done.

Under the "it's best to be prepared" theory I would like to outline a few steps

Other Catfishes with Axillary Glands

Axillary glands have been reported in catfishes of the families Ariidae, Ictaluridae, and Plotosidae. It's reasonable to assume that additional catfishes will be found to possess a similar system as more species are discovered, studied, and indentified. But the importance, or lack thereof, of this structure in venom production still awaits the results of studies that are currently underway.

to follow should you receive a catfish spine injury. This is not intended as medical advice, but should be taken as a general first aid approach to the topic.

Soak the Injury: If you experience an injury from a spine, the first thing that should be done is to soak the affected part in hot water. The water should at least be around 110°F (43°C), or even hotter if you can stand it. Heat tends to denature the venom.

Seek Help: If the pain is persistent, and especially if it starts to move (i.e., up the arm with a hand injury), you should seek medical assistance. Hopefully, you will have remembered which type of catfish was involved, and you should pass this information along to your doctor. Doctors may not be at all familiar with catfishes, but with the medical materials available through the Internet they should be able to check for any specific information that has been published. I have personally researched the topic through the medical library of a hospital at which I worked, and I can attest to such availability of materials.

If your initial pain goes away rather quickly (within an hour or two) but subsequently you develop any signs of an infection, such as pressure, pain, increasing redness, warmth in the area, etc., you should seek medical attention. Secondary infections are not uncommon with catfish wounds. Numerous bacteria might be associated with such

The commonly available shark catfish is capable of delivering a nasty sting with its sharp fins.

cases—*Aeromonas* is one of the most problematic for freshwater catfishes. In saltwater species, as might happen with a coral cat sting, *Vibrio* infections are prevalent. Such infections can be quite serious and demand immediate treatment.

Embedded Spine: Subsequent to the initial wound's healing, if there's any pain or swelling without signs of infection, it's advisable to see your doctor, because this could be indicative of an embedded piece of catfish spine. This can be determined by an X-ray. Such material can cause a foreign-body reaction, so it should be investigated fully.

You Never Know

While all of this information may paint some catfishes in a negative way, it's not meant to do so. It's only here to make you aware of one of the potential problems in keeping and handling catfishes. This is an area that should be considered by all keepers of catfishes—just in case.

Food and Feeding

There are numerous aspects involving the successful aquarium management of catfishes. One of the most important is providing a proper nutritious and balanced diet. On one level this can be fairly easy, because many catfishes can live, grow, and even reproduce on a diet of commercially prepared dry foods. But their captive lives can be improved by providing, in addition to commercially prepared foods, a wide variety of items more closely approximating the foods that they would eat in nature. I strongly believe that commercially available foods, with their wide variety of ingredients (including added vitamins and minerals), should be offered to any catfish that will eat them, but there are many other foods that should also be regularly included.

With that said, let's take a look at the various potential foods for catfishes.

Many loricariid catfish, such as this *Ancistrus* species feed by scraping algae off submerged surfaces in their home waters.

Algae

Algae in aquaria has often been viewed as a problem. However, for aquarists who maintain algae-eating catfishes, such as species of the genera *Otocinclus, Ancistrus, Hypostomus*, etc., it's the *lack* of algae that may be viewed as a problem. While many commercial foods contain algae and other green matter, offering live algae to algae-eating fishes is recommended. Such algae can add additional nutrients to the diet of these catfishes and also allows them to go about their natural grazing way of feeding. (Not all loricariids are algae eaters. For more on this, see Chapter 5.) Many other catfishes, such as some *Corydoras* and *Synodontis* species, will also enjoy grazing on natural algae, albeit with less efficiency and gusto than the more algae-dependent species.

There are some techniques that aquarists can use to provide a regular or at least semi-regular supply of live algae to their catfishes. Two of these techniques are based on the concept of movable feeding platforms.

Decor

If you have a few tanks and keep only a single loricariid catfish or two in one tank, you can consider rotating algae-laden tank furniture, such as driftwood, rocks, and commercial decorations from the non-catfish tanks into the tank with the catfishes.

They will love the snack and provide you with a cleaned object. You can then return the objects to their home tank(s) to grow more algae. In using this method, you just want to be sure that both (or all) tanks are free of any health problems. This method will do nothing for algae that grow on the glass, so you might have to do a little scrubbing yourself—at least on the inside of the front glass. Having some algae on the side and back glass isn't a problem and will be helpful in providing supplemental biological filtration to the tank. But some aquarists don't like the look of this and would rather have it all gone. So, instead of rotating furniture, you can rotate algae-eating catfishes. Again, assuming that all tanks are healthy, just introduce the cats to the new tank as you would introduce any other new fish to avoid any potential for shock.

Grow Your Own

Another way of providing algae is to grow it outdoors. This is the best method if you have a good population of algae-eating catfishes. In the best seasons for growth in my area (I am in a northern latitude) I set up containers outside in full sun, fill them with water, and add a variety of platform objects. Almost any larger container can be used; I've found rigid foam fish boxes ideal for this. The algae will then do what they do best—grow. You can speed things up with seeding the containers by scrubbing off an algae-covered object or two from an aquarium in the container's water. As the algae grow you can rotate the objects through your tanks. A word of caution: outdoor containers of water will no doubt attract mosquitoes that will lay their eggs in them. Luckily, fish love mosquito larvae. Regularly harvest the larvae with a fine-weave net and use the larvae as an excellent live food for many of the smaller, faster catfishes (auchenipterids, bagrids, etc.). Or you can freeze them in a small amount of water and use as you will for a greater variety of catfishes. If you don't want to be regularly chasing mosquito larvae, you can keep a few adult guppies in your algae vats. This will pretty well guarantee a lack of mosquito larvae and a population of healthy,

Cory cats will feed on algae, although they are not particularly specialized to do so.

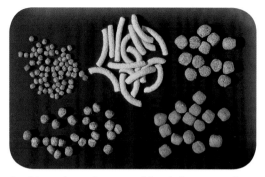

A wide variety of prepared foods is appropriate for catfish. Varieties that have a high algae content are especially good.

well-fed guppies. You might want to use some of the guppies as food for smaller to medium-sized predatory catfishes.

Dry Prepared Foods

This grouping includes such foods as flakes, pellets, sticks, wafers, tablets, crumbles, and so on. Some of these foods are also commonly available in both floating and sinking styles, which is useful because different catfishes have different feeding styles.

One can easily be overwhelmed by the variety of such foods and the fact that new ones are being added on a regular basis. They are many times formulated, and specifically advertised, for a particular fish or group of fishes. Notable among these are formulas that are specifically marketed for loricariids. Such foods usually have a high algae content and many contain a variety of other vegetable-based ingredients. But don't think that this food should be limited to the specific catfishes it targets. Many, if not most, catfishes regularly ingest at least some vegetal material, so such foods have a wide potential use. Keep in mind that even purely predatory catfishes end up eating what their prey has eaten. So a catfish, such as a pimelodid, that eats a small fish that has been feeding on plants or detritus will get the nutritional benefit of those foods as the prey is digested. The same concept works for catfishes that feed predominately on invertebrates, many of which eat plant material.

Keep the various commercial foods in a relatively cool and dry place. A fishroom is *not* an ideal place for such foods. Should you purchase these foods in bulk, it's good to divide them up and store a large part in a freezer. A container that has a tight lid that can be burped is ideal. But remember that even under frozen conditions some nutrients will be lost over a period of time. So sometimes you might want to reduce the size of your bulk food purchases..

Feeder Fishes

There are quite a few catfishes that will benefit from the addition of small live fishes to their diet. Although many predatory catfishes will often adapt to a diet of other meaty foods, the feeding of small live fishes should be considered at least on an occasional

Provide Several Options

No one dry prepared food should be considered as sufficient for feeding your catfishes. Although modern fish food technology is constantly creating improved new products with greater stability, it's wise to offer a variety of such foods to help guarantee a good nutritional profile. Small amounts of two or more foods can be fed simultaneously, and you can mix and match with the various available formats (flake, pellets, wafers, etc.) to see which your catfishes prefer.

basis. These add the thrill of the chase to the feeding experience and can provide additional needed nutrients. If you're going to feed such foods to your catfishes there are a few things that should be considered.

Feeders May Be Dangerous

Most feeder fishes, including guppies, goldfish, and the so-called tuffies, are usually kept in large numbers in small quarters, so there's always the potential that they might harbor some problems (bacterial diseases, parasites, etc.). Closely examine any such fishes before purchasing them. If any problems, such as bloody bodies or fins, fungus or ich, excessive respiration, hanging at the surface (or lying on the bottom), etc., are evident, pass those fishes by.

Even if the feeder fishes seem fine, to just purchase them and then put them directly into your home tank can be a disaster waiting to happen. In doing this you will eventually introduce an unwanted problem into your happily running tank.

A Feeder Tank

If you're going to offer live fishes, it's best to set up a small tank (a 10-gallon [40-liter] tank will be fine) and treat the feeder fish as well as you would any others, including regular feedings with a variety of foods. This allows you to have a quarantine time to observe the feeder fishes and make sure that you aren't going to introduce any problems into your other tank(s).

Once your feeders are judged to be free of problems and have settled into their tank, be sure to feed them well with a good brand of flake food shortly before offering them to your catfishes. This is called gut loading and provides an extra nutritional boost to whatever fish eats them.

Cultivate Your Own Feeders

If you have room for a tank for your feeders, you can raise your own feeder fishes. Set up a separate tank with a working biofilter, a substrate, and plants. Feed the fishes and change the tank's water regularly. You can breed and raise your own guppies, gouramis, convict cichlids—whatever you can breed in sufficient quantity. And the best part is you don't have to fear exposing your main tank to.any diseases; well-raised feeders should be healthy and free of any illnesses.

Large catfishes, such as the tiger shovelnose, will eagerly eat feeder fish, but it is best to provide them a varied diet.

Use Smaller Feeders

Feeder fishes should be proportional to the size of the catfishes that are being fed. While a larger feeder fish might be a better value, it may also provide digestive challenges. Smaller fishes lessen the chance that the food might be regurgitated, which can happen with large fish meals. It's far better to use smaller goldfish, or better yet feeder guppies or tuffies, if you are going to use this food source. Also, don't over-feed the catfishes just because smaller fishes are being used. The feeding of too many smaller fishes at one time, which predatory fishes will often eat to excess if they are available, may lead to regurgitation, with resultant degrading of the water quality.

Freeze-Dried and Frozen Foods

Freeze-dried and frozen foods are commonly available, but there are certain aspects to them that you must be aware of.

Freeze-Dried Foods

Freeze-dried foods come with their own feeding situation. By virtue of their processing method, these foods will float. With many catfishes this isn't a problem; they will, as they often do in nature, rise to the surface to feed. These foods will, upon being eaten, reconstitute and expand. So in general terms you don't want to overload your catfishes with such foods, as it may cause serious health problems.

Special consideration must be used with freeze-dried foods for catfishes that will not come to the surface to feed. You can soak the food in a container of tap water, but this alone isn't sufficient to allow a reasonable amount of the food to become reconstituted and sink. In this kind of situation you can gently press the floating freeze-dried food between your fingers to help it absorb water, thus making it sinkable. With most freeze-dried foods you will never get it all completely sinkable, but by getting a good amount of the food to absorb enough water for it to sink and then doing a quick tap water rinse before adding to the tank, you can help to guarantee that both surface feeders and those more closely tied to the bottom will get their share of food equally. If you have very aggressive eaters that will go for food on both the surface and in mid-water, you might need another feeding strategy. (More on this in a moment.)

Frozen Foods

If you follow most package directions, offering the various frozen foods sounds very straightforward. You simply break off a piece, or if it's one of the multiple individual servings in a pack, you punch it out into the tank. The piece, or portion(s), then defrost and/or melt and the catfishes eat it. But, as with many things, it's not necessarily so simple. Many catfishes will eagerly attack the food even before it has a chance to break up. In fact, some larger catfishes may just gulp the still-frozen food right down.

Also, while some frozen foods are relatively clean, others may not be. For example, there are some brine shrimp products that will release a large amount of brownish liquid into the tank. This is of organic origin and will add to the bioload in your

A Catfish Feeding Regimen

As with all foods, except some of the natural foods for grazing catfishes, it's best to feed moderately and avoid overfeeding. Nature tells fishes to eat when the eating is good, but with the aquarist in charge a regular supply of food is guaranteed. Do your best not to overfeed your catfishes. One method you can employ that will help make sure they aren't being fed too much is to designate one day per week as a fast day—don't offer your fishes any food. Fast days keep your fishes healthy and also help your tank's biological filtration from being overwhelmed.

Bloodworms are the larvae of certain species of midges and make a nutritious addition to a catfish's diet. While they are sometimes available live, more often they are sold frozen or freeze-dried.

aquarium. As a little test, take a 2-inch by 2-inch (5 x 5-cm) section off a frozen block of brine shrimp and let it melt into a container of cold tap water. When this is done, stir up the brine shrimp. You might be surprised how brown the formerly clear water will be. (You can also get reddish water if you do the same with bloodworms.) Adding this biological-based coloration to your tank, especially over a period of time, is not good and will necessitate additional water changes.

One school of thought, and certainly to some degree a valid one, is that if you melt your frozen foods in water and then rinse them in a tight-mesh net under cold water before feeding, you will lose some of the nutrient quality of the food (vitamins especially). This will be even more the case with foods to which additional nutrients have been added during the preparing and freezing processes. With brine shrimp, if you purchase some of the cleaner formulas in which the additional nutrient materials have been fed to the shrimp prior to freezing, this will be less of a problem.

So you must make a decision. I personally prefer the melt-rinse-feed method, because any loss of quality with this method can be overcome by offering the generally more stable dry foods—and all of that brown/red organic water is not going into my tanks.

Natural Meaty Foods

A good part of the natural diet of many wild catfishes consists of a wide variety of meaty items. Most notable among these foods are insects (larvae, pupae, and adults), various crustaceans, and mollusks. Even many predatory catfishes that might normally feed mainly on other fishes in the wild will accept many of the commercial meaty foods that are available.

Many such foods are available in a number of formats, such as live, frozen, or freeze-dried. Which of them you choose can depend on a number of factors: cost, convenience, availability, and the feeding preferences of your catfishes.

Bloodworms

Bloodworms are insects, the larvae of non-biting midges. There are hardly any catfishes that will not eat bloodworms at one time or another during their life. For the primarily insectivorous catfish species, bloodworms are a natural and prime dietary item. The bloodworms that are commercially available are generally nutritious and a good source of protein. When purchasing frozen bloodworms, look for those with a nice reddish coloration. They will have received better care and preparation than the sometimes seen more grayish-appearing product. Live bloodworms may be available in your local stores, but this is the most expensive way to procure them.

Brine shrimp, *Artemia* spp.

Adult brine shrimp are the most widely used natural meaty type of food item. Like bloodworms, they're available as both frozen and freeze-dried products. Some brands of frozen brine shrimp are enriched. This is done either by adding substances (vitamins, etc.) to the product when it's frozen or by offering special foods to the brine shrimp as they grow and immediately prior to harvesting.

Brine shrimp are also available in egg form. The eggs can be hatched for live feeding to a wide variety of mostly smaller catfishes. If you're trying to breed your catfishes, newly hatched shrimp can be a beneficial food in the initial stages of raising baby catfishes.

Warning: Allergies

I must note here that there are some potential problems with bloodworms for a small number of aquarists. Some hobbyists have had an allergic reaction after handling them. Should this be the case it would be best to avoid their use—especially the freeze-dried version, which exudes bloodworm dust.

Enriched Adult Brine Shrimp Only

Adult brine shrimp by themselves, without enrichment of any kind, are a good food, but far from excellent. It would be better to use one of the enriched brine shrimp products to maximize nutritional quality. If you use regular (non-enriched) brine shrimp, a number of liquid-based products can be added to the shrimp prior to feeding. This technique will work with both frozen and freeze-dried products, but it should be more effective on the latter due to better absorption.

Baby brine shrimp, often in an enriched formula, are also available in frozen form and will be eaten by many of the same catfishes.

Gammarus spp.

Gammarus are small freshwater amphipods (a type of crustacean) that are often mistakenly called shrimp. They are most commonly available as either a freeze-dried or sun-dried product. You may find them offered as a turtle food, but they make a great addition to the diet of most catfishes that prefer meaty items. *Gammarus* don't have as great an attractant smell as many other foods, so you should offer them along with a pinch of a good flake food to get the catfish's attention. Like bloodworms, but to a lesser extent, allergic responses have been reported from use of this product.

Krill

Although these shrimp-like crustaceans are marine in origin, they are good for freshwater catfishes in modest amounts. Krill, and the smaller forms sold as "plankton," are a very nutritious food, rich in protein, vitamin A, and carotenoids, which can help enhance the colors of the catfishes that are fed it.

Other Meaty Foods

The previous four food items only scratch the surface in regard to commercially available meaty foods. Some other potentials that should be considered as part of a rotating food program include: blackworms, daphnia, mysis shrimps, glassworms, mosquito larvae, tubifex worms, redworms, and snails (pond and aquarium species). Crushed snails will be greedily fed upon by many catfishes. Live snails can also be used as food for many species of medium-size to large catfishes. A number of doradid catfishes (*Megalodoras uranoscopus, Pterodoras granulosus*, etc.) will swallow them whole. Some *Synodontis* species will swallow smaller snails whole, while *S. multipunctata* (and probably the co-existing *S. grandiops*) will grab the snail and jerk it from its shell before eating it.

A Meaty Food to Avoid

There is one last group of meaty foods that I would suggest not using at all: products that consist totally, or predominately, of beef heart. Overall, the digestive systems of catfishes have not evolved to be able to adequately handle mammalian meat and its fatty content.

Vegetables

When one thinks of vegetables as food for catfishes, the South American loricariids will most likely come to mind. Within this group, many genera and species are well known for their algae-eating abilities, and this green tooth will transition to other vegetal foods. But loricariids aren't the only catfishes that will accept various vegetables as food. I have worked with a variety of such foods on an equal variety of catfishes. Fresh vegetables are commonly used, but both canned and frozen varieties are also options. Every catfish may not like every vegetable, but *Synodontis* species, *Corydoras* species, various doradids, more than a few auchenipterids, and many others have feasted on vegetables as a part of their captive diet. Even adult

Other Possible Foods for Your Catfishes

When it comes to selecting food items for your catfishes, don't think you're limited to one aisle in your local pet store. There are a number of natural foods (often enriched with vitamins and minerals) consisting of small laboratory-raised flies, crickets (adult and young), grasshoppers, and mealworms (larvae of certain beetles) that are produced for lizard and turtle food that you can offer to your catfishes. These animals are well worth considering as additional food items. Some are available as dried products, while others are canned, requiring subsequent refrigeration.

There are also various frozen commercial seafood-based products that can be fed in modest amounts to freshwater catfishes. These include mussels, squid, scallops, and fish such as whole silversides.

There's also a reasonable selection of frozen foods containing a variety of ingredients that you can buy. These foods are often targeted towards a certain fish or group of fishes (discus, Malawi cichlids, etc.). Although they are often a bit more expensive, they make for a nice occasional treat. Just check the ingredients and see what might fit your needs.

predators such as *Ageneiosus magoi* (which in the wild feeds primarily on insects, fishes, and frogs) have been known to enjoy the occasional lightly boiled zucchini.

How to Offer Vegetables

There are two schools of thought in regard to feeding vegetables to catfishes. The first is to feed them in a raw state. The second is to lightly boil them (microwaving also works). I fall within the second group. The exceptions to this are some leafy produce that don't respond well to boiling water.

The primary advantages to a light one-minute-or-so boil are that: 1) the boiled vegetables will readily sink in the aquarium, whereas much raw produce will float and consequently need to be held down by one method or another; and 2) a light boil breaks down some of the cellulose, thus allowing an increased availability of many of the contained nutrients. Some vitamins may be somewhat diminished by this light boiling, but overall the effect is positive. Zucchini can serve as an example. If it's sliced into quarter- to half-inch rounds and then boiled for a minute, it can then be frozen on cookie sheets and stored in plastic freezer containers. These rounds can then be removed as needed and dropped into the aquarium, where they'll defrost and sink. If you're using round slices it's good to make a complete lengthwise cut, either with your thumbnail or a small knife, in the skin so that when the middle is eaten away you will have a strip of skin instead of a ring. I, and others, have had loricariids get fatally tangled up in these tough skin rings.

The striped Raphael catfish is but one of many species that will eat vegetables.

Raw zucchini can be sliced, either into rounds or lengthwise, and then it must be attached to a heavier object to hold it down. The attachment can ideally be done with a clean rubber band or some other method of your choice.

No matter which method you use for zucchini (or another vegetable) you will generally have the initial situation of leftover skins. Zucchini skins are a great source of vitamin

A. However, your grazing catfishes will not have much interest in the skin at first, just the softer middle parts. They will eventually return to the skins if no other foods are offered.

Good Starter Vegetables

When it comes to other vegetables, it's good to experiment. Don't give up too soon; give your catfish(es) a chance to adapt

Many aquarists feed zucchini to their catfishes, and you can offer many other vegetables as well.

to new foods. To encourage this you can cut back on their regular favorites a bit to leave them a little hungry. As long as they're in good condition this won't create any problems. Some choices for initial vegetable items follow. Just take it easy, don't put too much in the tank, and observe what happens. Some foods will go fast—others a bit slower. From here, feel free to try other vegetables.

Beans: Regular green beans are a favorite of mine and my catfishes. I usually use the already cooked and canned varieties. The beans can be removed from the can, rinsed in cold water, stored in water in the refrigerator, and added to the tank. They will be appreciated by many catfishes. If you're breeding and raising up some loricariid catfishes, such as *Ancistrus* and *Rineloricaria*, the French-cut beans are a better choice, as they are softer and more easily eaten. Combined with some baby brine shrimp and some crushed flakes, these beans are an excellent starter food for such fishes.

Broccoli: This vegetable is rich in many nutrients, including vitamins A, C, and a number of B-complex vitamins. Additionally there many important minerals present. For catfishes, the main feeding parts of these vegetable are the stalks. The stalks can be fed raw after being washed in cold water, but a brief boiling can be beneficial by slightly softening up this somewhat tougher part of the vegetable. The flowerets are also nutritious, but since they're composed of numerous small pieces, they can make a mess when they're browsed upon.

Leafy Greens: Many of the darker green leafy vegetables are appreciated by loricariids. Other catfishes will often take to the "crumbs" that may be left after the plecos have done their work. Items like iceberg lettuce should generally be avoided, as they aren't particularly nutritious. Darker items like romaine, red leaf lettuce, and spinach are better choices. You can also consider bok (or pak) choy, which is often sold as Chinese cabbage. Pieces can be fed raw, after a good washing in cold water (if you think you're noticing a pattern with this, you are; all fresh vegetables should be given the same treatment). You might also want to consider blanching or even steaming them to increase the availability of certain nutrients. These items can be rubber banded to driftwood or some other platform, or held in place by the commercially available lettuce or seaweed clips.

Squashes: Zucchini was already mentioned, but don't overlook other types of squash such as butternut, yellow, etc.

Wood

Yes, wood. Basically, members of three genera of loricariids are involved:

- *Panaque*, including *P. nigrolineatus* (royal pleco), and *P. cochliodon* (blue-eye pleco).
- *Panaqolus,* which includes seven species, the best known of which is *Panaqolus maccus*. These are smaller fishes considered by some to just be a clade, or grouping, of small *Panaque* species.
- The so-called *Hypostomus cochliodon* group of the genus *Hypostomus*. About 16 species are currently assigned to this group. Earlier-described species were often placed in the genus *Cochliodon*, a name still subscribed to by some authorities.

In any case, all of these catfishes have similar dental equipment that enables them to rasp away chips of wood, which are then swallowed and digested. The dentition consists of two V-shaped groups of a few

If you are keeping species of *Panaque*, include some wood for them to graze on in the aquarium.

Wood for Your Tank

Even if you don't have any of the wood-eating loricariids, the presence of wood in the catfish aquarium is always a bonus. Many of the more generalist-feeding loricariids (*Ancistrus*, *Otocinclus*, etc.) will eagerly browse on the biocover (periphyton) that will naturally develop on the wood. After some wood has been in the aquarium for a few weeks you can note a slightly slimy feel to its surface. This is natural and is the appreciated food source. Other catfishes, such as *Corydoras* and *Synodontis* species, will also be seen making use of this natural supplemental food source.

strong teeth. The relatively large individual teeth are spoon-shaped and highly effective at scraping off small chips of wood. There may be some variation in the tooth structure; for example, some species of the *H. cochliodon* group that eat a lesser amount of wood have teeth that are less highly modified.

As far as is known, all of these catfishes show positive growth results from eating certain woods. What is known of the natural diets of some of the species (based on examining gut contents) shows that they also eat a variety of other foods. These included various algae, higher plants, detritus (broken down plant matter), sediment (including mud, sand, and associated microinvertebrates such as rotifers and protozoans), and insects (larvae and various unidentified parts). A good amount of such items are commonly found together, combined from a number of species, but it does clearly show a wide range of natural food sources for these catfishes. And some of them, in fact, had no wood in their digestive tracts at all.

So from this it's clear that members of *Panaque, Panaqolus,* and the *H. cochliodon* group should, in addition to wood, be fed a varying diet consisting of good amounts of prepared foods rich in vegetal content, natural vegetables, algae, and a small amount of meaty foods.

Which Woods to Offer

Even before the wood-eating situation was known scientifically, aquarists had observed that pieces of driftwood in the tank would slowly disappear from tanks holding the now-known wood-eating species. By their natural feeding method *Panaque* spp. will go at just about any piece of wood that's offered to them. Some of the commercially available sinking woods, such as Malaysian driftwood and Mopani wood, are ideal for use with these catfishes. The latter wood is particularly hard, but this doesn't seem to deter *Panaque* spp., especially larger individuals. These woods will leach tannins into the aquarium water and can make it quite dark, often with an accompanying drop in pH, so it's good to pre-soak them for a period of time to lessen this impact. Some use of boiling water in the soaking process will often speed up the process.

On Feeding Catfishes

Once they're settled into a given aquarium, most catfishes will not be shy when fed. But there are certain factors that you must keep in mind. These include, but are not necessarily limited to, the feeding styles of their tankmates (catfish and noncatfish) and the feeding styles, and levels of gregariousness, of the individual catfishes.

Dealing With Excess Food

If all of your fishes have had their fill there's always the chance of there being some uneaten leftovers, and this isn't good. It will begin to decompose and will degrade the water quality. Should you see such a situation, just siphon out the excess food. You'll have to add back new, fresh, and treated water to replace what was removed, but you can never get enough water changes.

Try Several Small Meals

In general principle I don't subscribe to any particular formula for how much food to offer at a particular feeding. This belief leaves out the various grazing catfishes who can be provided with vegetal foods (live algae, real vegetables) to eat constantly. For other catfishes, I prefer to feed a number of smaller meals throughout the day and evening. Your life schedule will have an effect on this, but ideally if you can feed two to four smaller meals a day it will be a much more natural way of eating for your catfishes. This even goes for the more predatory types that might be receiving some small live fishes.

Mix Things Up

When I feed I also like to mix up foods a bit instead of just using one food item. For example, if you're using a flake food, which tends to sink slowly, you might also offer some commercial granules, pellets, or discs, which will sink faster. This will help to assure that catfishes feeding at the top, middle, and bottom of the tank will get their fair share of food.

I also like to use this technique when offering meaty foods. I will mix frozen brine shrimp and bloodworms and offer these together. This helps make a healthier meal. I also will mix in a bit of flakes too.

Targeted Feedings

If you have some shy catfishes who don't respond well to feeding times during the day you might try some targeted feeding. Some of the catfishes that often tend to be slower or a bit shy (banjo cats come to mind) may not easily come out of their hiding places. If you have an idea where the shy catfishes are hiding you can deliver whatever foods you're using directly to them with the use of a small food baster or one of the larger baby animal feeding droppers that are available.

While a great majority of catfishes are generally thought of as nocturnal, this isn't the whole story. There are definitely some that are more light-shy than others and this needs to be considered when feeding. Consequently, it's a good idea to do at least one feeding at night after the lights in the aquarium have been out for a while. In a more general community situation most of the fishes will respond to the dark by hiding away and/or sleeping. This will allow the catfishes, especially those that might be more shy, to come out and eat.

Observe Your Catfishes

There are no hard and set rules on how and when to feed your catfishes. Although they are a highly diverse group, many will easily fall into whatever feeding schedule you set up. But there are always going to be a few that may not readily fit into such a plan. Observe your catfishes closely and see what they like to eat and when they like to eat it. A little observation can go a long way in guaranteeing a healthy and well-fed catfish.

You may need to use targeted feedings to be sure shy species, such as banjo cats, are getting enough food.

Health Care

Catfishes, like all other aquarium fishes, are subject to a number of potential health problems. Many of these problems, especially among wild-caught catfishes, often occur soon after the fishes have been purchased. This is due to a number of factors, including the stress that such catfishes have been subjected to in the capture, holding, and shipping phases needed to get them to your local store. Additionally, during this time they are may be subjected to fluctuating temperatures, multiple water quality differences, and exposure to many other fishes or the water they were in. All of the parties involved in bringing catfishes to you do their best to prevent the spread of problems, but sometimes things just happen.

As noted in Chapter 1, the best way to treat any problems with new purchases is to have a quarantine procedure in place. This isolates new acquisitions, making them easier to observe and treat if any problems show up.

Water Quality

Maintaining good water quality is the first line of defense in preventing health problems. This goes not only for your quarantine tank but also for your more permanent setups as well. Maintaining good water quality starts with providing optimal filtration systems, including both mechanical and biological filtration. The first removes particulate material from the water. The second manages the nitrogen cycle and converts ammonia to nitrite and then nitrite to nitrate. There are numerous choices among different products that provide both types of filtration, and they are often combined. Research different brands to find which ones are best for your needs.

Water Changes

Mechanical and biological filtration is necessary for success, but more is needed. You can use some of the products available that provide additional removal of organics and other substances, but you cannot beat partial water changes for maintaining the quality of your water. This is true also as regards nitrate, which though less toxic to fishes than ammonia and nitrite does become a problem when it accumulates to high levels. Water changing involves the removal of a certain percentage of the tank's water and replacing it with fresh water treated to remove chlorine or chloramine. To remove water from your tank you should use a wide-mouth siphon that doubles as a gravel vacuum. This removes built-up organic matter that can degrade your water.

Good water quality is your first line of defense against disease in your aquarium, and good water quality demands performing regular partial water changes.

How much water to change? That depends on the organic load on the tank. Predatory catfishes that eat a lot of meaty foods will of course create a lot of nitrogen-based waste. But loricariids that are constantly eating vegetal material will also generate quite a lot of waste.

As a starting point, I like to recommend a 25- to 30-percent weekly water change for catfish tanks. This is predicated on the assumption that both filtration concepts (mechanical and biological) are in maximal working order. If you have catfishes that produce a lot of waste, or just a tank with a very heavy population, you might even consider a higher percentage of weekly change, say 35 to 40 percent. But try to avoid going below the 25- to 30-percent range.

If you slack off on water changes, you may start to see differences in the behavior and physical condition of the catfishes. They can become sluggish.

Randomly distributed white spots on a fish usually indicates an ich infestation. This can be difficult to see on the catfish like this one that naturally have white spots.

They may rub up against edges in the tank, and their appetites will often be diminished. Many times the eyes might cloud up, and there will be an increase in body slime production. Additionally, colors may often fade. These symptoms are sometimes taken as "sickness" and followed up with medication. This will only add unnecessary stress to the situation. What is needed first is a good partial water change, or a series of changes over a few days, accompanied by a full diagnostic on your filtration systems to bring them up to optimal levels. If all of this isn't done, a medical situation can develop—creating a real and serious problem.

Common Diseases

Medical problems that can affect catfishes, often bacterial or parasitic in origin, should be closely watched for during the quarantine period. Once properly identified they will need to be treated—this will lengthen the quarantine time.

A couple of general considerations should be taken into consideration before you begin a disease treatment procedure. If a disease problem, real or potential, is noted and a treatment is elected, you should, before starting treatment, change about 25 percent of the water so that the environment is freshened up. Also, remove carbon or any other medication-removing product that might be present in the filter or tank. If you add a medication to water being treated with carbon, the carbon will adsorb it, preventing it from treating the fish. These basics go for both regular and quarantine tanks.

Bacteria

Bacterial problems may display themselves as a grayish-whitish coating on the body; often there may be fraying and disintegration on the edges of the fins. There may also be small bloody spots or streaks on the body. Should such changes be noted you should administer an antibiotic treatment. Over the years I personally have had very good results with furan-based antibiotics, but there are many other useful products available at your aquarium store. Whichever product you choose, be sure to follow the manufacturer's directions exactly.

Fungus

One problem that can be seen with catfishes from time to time is the presence of fungal tufts on the ends of the dorsal or pectoral spines. This is an opportunistic infection resulting from damage to the end of the spines; it's usually initiated by having the spines get caught and damaged in a netting episode.

   Medication is sold to take care of such situations, but in the absence of any other problems I don't like to medicate an entire tank for such a localized problem. My suggested way of dealing with this situation is: net the catfish (in a tight-weave net) and take a small piece of clean wet cloth and swab at the fungal area. Do this on the top and bottom of the fish's spine. This should remove the fungus. Often this is all that's needed. But to be sure I prefer to swab the affected area of the fin with a small amount of either acriflavin or methylene blue to kill any trace of fungus that might remain. Keep in mind that it's during such handling of catfishes that spine wounds to the hand may occur. (See Chapter 1.)

Parasites

The most commonly seen parasitic disease is ich, or white spot. This is caused by the ciliated protozoan *Ichthyophthirius multifiliis,* which manifests itself as small white spots scattered over the fish's body and fins. While in this cyst-like form the parasite cannot be easily killed; treatment is effective only after the parasite has left the host fish and

Ich Medications

There are numerous medications on the market for ich, but you have to be very careful in regard to which of them you use on catfishes. The standard ich medication has long consisted of malachite green, and this can be a real problem for catfishes, often killing or severely damaging them when used at the suggested standard doses. So great care is needed in treating catfishes with ich! Luckily there are a number of formulas on the market that are aimed specifically at the treatment of scaleless fishes such as catfishes. Seek these medications out at your local store and carefully follow the provided directions. You might also talk with store personnel and other aquarists to learn of their experiences with the use of similar medications.

formed cysts from which new young parasites—the free-swimming form of this pesty protozoan—soon emerge. Before starting treatment, do a large water change (about 40 percent)—this will physically remove many of the free-swimming forms, which will make treatment easier. Most often it's recommended that the tank's temperature be raised by a few degrees, as this will speed up the parasite's life cycle. In principle this is good, but keep a close eye on the fish. Higher temperatures might cause them some breathing stress—the gills are probably also affected by the parasites. Adding some additional aeration to the tank may help with this.

Your Fish Will Get Sick

Eventually most aquarists will end up with health problems of one type or another with their catfishes. It's the nature of the beast. But by working towards quarantine procedures and optimal water quality in all tanks, illnesses and infections will most often be kept at bay. And when a problem does occur, quick action using proper products will lessen the impact on the catfish—and the hobbyist.

4

Breeding

The captive breeding of catfishes, all of which are egg layers, is a pursuit to be encouraged. Basic knowledge regarding the reproduction of a great number of catfishes is lacking, and aquarists can help to provide valuable information. Additionally, the pressures of commercial collecting on at least some wild populations can be reduced. In other cases there may be subsequent restrictions on collecting . A good example is the situation with the popular *Hypancistrus zebra* from the Rio Xingu in Brazil. This beautiful catfish was collected in large numbers throughout the late 1980s, 90s, and the early 2000s. Now this species is listed as endangered by Brazil, and exports are prohibited. So we hobbyists are left to work with what fish we have. Luckily, there's a reasonable amount of captive breeding being done by hobbyists with this species. If for any reason these captive-breeding populations should disappear, this popular and attractive species could be lost to the hobby forever. In many ways the future of the catfish hobby is in the hands of hobbyists.

Hypancistrus zebra has become an endangered species and is now only available as captive-spawned stock.

The Best Spawners

From the point of aquarium successes in breeding catfishes, the genus *Corydoras* certainly leads the way. A great majority of the 150 or so described species (and numerous undescribed species) have been bred. Some formerly rare and expensive wild-caught fishes are now available as multi-generation, tank-raised fish at reasonable prices. The same can be said for many loricariids.

Once we get beyond these two families the number of aquarium-spawned species becomes more limited. But increasingly more is happening in this area, and information on such events is becoming more widely available. The Internet has played a major role in the dispersal of such information.

So You Want to Spawn Your Catfishes

For a spawning project, information about whether and how a species has been spawned should be sought out and reviewed. This background research can often be very helpful. If you cannot find anything on the particular species, try to find information on others belonging to the same genus. And if you can't find even this, just experiment…and keep notes!

Purchasing With Intent to Breed

If a species you want to spawn has already being spawned in captivity you can purchase a group of juveniles, raise them up together to maturity, and let nature take its course. This is a good method in that it gives you plenty of time to work with and study the particular catfish. It can also be more economical, since you can often obtain a large number of tank-bred juveniles for what a few wild-caught adult fish might cost. The only drawback is the amount of time needed to raise the young fish. Depending on the species involved, this might range from eight or nine months to two or two and a half years.

In purchasing larger wild-caught catfish for a breeding attempt, you will also be faced with some choices. With some of the smaller and less expensive species it isn't a real problem to obtain a group of say four to six individuals and take it from there. Many such catfishes aren't going to be easy to initially sex (especially newly imported stock at a store), but after conditioning in your home tank this can often be done with a good level of assuredness. Another method for choosing breeding stock from among wild-caught individuals is to pick out a pair or pairs or other combinations where sexing is possible. There are quite a few forms of sexual dimorphism (noticeable differences between males and females) among the catfishes, and you should familiarize yourself with those differences.

Corydoras species have been bred in captivity long enough to produce many generations of aquarium-adapted fishes. Breeders have also developed color varieties, such as these albino reds.

One Pair Versus Multiple Pairs

Obtaining just one pair of a particular species does carry risk. If one of the partners dies, you are then left with only one fish, and it might be difficult to obtain another suitable mate. So if you're really interested in attempting to spawn a given species, it's best to try to obtain at least two pairs, especially if they can be easily sexed. You can hold one male in reserve and set up the other with two females—this is a good way to tone down and spread out the potential for male-on-female aggression that can be seen in some species. However, this only considers some parts of a situation where pair formation or just male/female (pair in the loose sense) mating may result in a spawning event that produces eggs. There are multiple ways that catfishes may spawn, and often a group dynamic is involved. For instance, it's possible to spawn just a single pair of a *Corydoras* species or a pair of *Synodontis multipunctata*. But with these species others present in the tank will often join in on the spawning. When they're in a group and spawning begins, every fish appears to get involved.

Good Starter Species

If you have never spawned a catfish and would like to do so, there are a few good species to start with. One of the commercially available *Corydoras* species, such as

A number of *Corydoras* species, such as *C. aeneus*, are relatively easy to spawn in the aquarium.

C. aeneus or *C. paleatus*, is ideal. You can work with any species, but these two have been raised successfully in captivity for a long time and are great starters. They are egg scatterers (or placers) that exhibit no further parental involvement.

Another ideal starter catfish is an *Ancistrus* species. This genus of loricariids contains, in my opinion, the best catfish species for an initial breeding experience. With these fishes, the male will set up territory in a cave or cave-like feature and coax a ripe female inside for spawning. After the eggs are laid, the female leaves. If there's more than one female in the tank, both (if ripe) will often lay eggs with the one male. The male takes charge and cares for the eggs until they hatch, and afterwards he continues with the care and defense of the fry. As the fry grow they will slowly spread away from the male's territory and develop their own lives. Meanwhile, the male is ready to spawn again.

Uncharted Territory

There is much to be done and learned with the captive breeding of catfishes. It's not a clean slate to work with, but it's one with a whole lot of empty space. The results and answers come slowly, but they are coming. Join up and fill in some blanks.

Ancistrus species are a good subject for first-time catfish breeders. Here a male *Ancistrus* sp. has enticed a female into his cave (top). After the female lays her eggs, she leaves and the male cares for them (center). The larvae initially stay in the male's cave, dispersing slowly (bottom).

Family Profiles

The aim of this chapter is to provide a brief overview of some families of catfishes and selected members of each family that might be considered as aquarium inhabitants. Size considerations for various species are listed as either standard length (SL) or total length (TL). Standard length doesn't include the caudal (tail) fin; total length does. For the most part, the structure of the families herein is based on the following publication: Ferraris Jr., C. J. 2007. Checklist of catfishes, recent and fossil (Osteichthys, Siluriformes), and catalogue of siluriform primary types. *Zootaxa* (1418), 628 pages. This excellent resource is available free of charge at www.mapress.com/zootaxa.

Amphilius atesuensis. Fish in the genus *Amphilius* appreciate cooler temperatures and moving water.

Akysidae

This is an interesting group of mainly Southeast Asian and Indonesian catfishes. Some, albeit rarely, are becoming more available to the hobby. There are five genera— *Acrochordonichthys, Akysis, Breitensteinia, Parakysis,* and *Pseudobagarius*—and around 50 species in the family.

Akysis and *Pseudobagarius* are small fishes not more than 2 inches (5 cm) SL. They're usually called bumblebee catfish in the trade but don't confuse them. Asian bagrids (e.g., *Pseudomystus siamensis*) that are also called this, and they get substantially larger. *Akysis* and *Pseudobagarius* superficially bear a resemblance to the small South American *Microglanis* species (family Pseudopimelodidae) in their color patterning, but the Asian bumblebees possess nasal barbels and their bodies bear numerous tubercles (round nodules). Along with the genus *Parakysis*, these fishes can deliver a very painful wound via their pectoral spines. Don't let the small size and nice colors lull you into being careless.

These genera are micropredators and feed on insect larvae and small shrimps, probably also on microinvertebrates. They are usually found in areas with at least some current, so this should be considered in setting up a tank for them. They need hiding places—the substrate can serve this purpose. If you provide them with sand they will spend a lot of their time buried in it. Water conditions can be a temperature slightly less than standard tropical, a pH of 6.5 to 7.0, and soft to low hardness.

The genus *Breitensteinia* is to me the most interesting of the group. Its species are elongate and strongly resemble large and long banjo catfishes. Like banjos, they too go through a regular skin-shedding process. There are three species in the genus, all from Sumatra and Borneo. They're known to eat small shrimps in the wild. I would assume that insect larvae are also a staple of the diet.

Amblycipitidae

This small family, known as torrent catfishes, has poor representation in the hobby. The 27 known species are placed in three genera. It appears that neither of the two Chinese species in the genus *Xiurenbagrus* have ever been imported as aquarium fishes. The status of another genus, *Liobagrus* as a provider of aquarium fishes also is in question. This genus has 12 described species found in China, Korea, and Japan.

The one genus seen from time to time in the hobby is *Amblyceps*, with 14 described species, and some of them have potential hobby availability from India, Myanmar (Burma), Thailand, and the upper Malay Peninsula. *Amblyceps* are smaller (generally under 4 inches [10 cm] SL) elongated catfishes that are sometimes described as loach-like. They typically are found in fast-flowing waters, a condition that should be matched by making sure that both current and additional aeration are offered.

Amphiliidae

This family, sometimes called loach or mountain catfishes, is widespread in Africa. Currently there are 75 species in 12 genera. Many of the species aren't well known to science, and future work will no doubt increase the number of both genera and species. Most amphiliids live in fast-flowing water at higher elevations. Some are found in streams at over 1 mile (1.6 km) above sea level. These habitats have a rocky substrate.

The rocky stream amphiliids can be divided into two main groups (subfamilies). The first group, consisting of two genera (*Amphilius* and *Paramphilius*), reaches around 4 to 6 inches (10 to 15 cm) SL. Their naked bodies are fairly thick-skinned and can have an almost rubbery look to them. These catfishes lack typical spines on their

Phractura ansorgii. Fish in the genus *Phractura* seem to feed primarily on insect larvae.

dorsal and pectoral fins, and the main holding ray is soft and rubbery. The undersides of the pectoral fins have many small projections that help hold the fish in place in its fastwater habitat. Some of these catfishes are rather plain, while others show variations of spotting, body saddles, lighter horizontal lines, etc.

Members of *Amphilius* are imported into the hobby from time to time. There are 24 species in this genus, but the ones we see can be counted on one hand. These fish appreciate cooler water and some directed current over the lower part of the tank, which can ideally be set up in a rocky jumble. In this way they are very much like the Asian *Amblyceps* and the South American *Astroblepus* species. *Amphilius* species will spend a lot of time hiding, but when foods are offered up they'll take it in a fast and hectic manner. They aren't fussy about foods, but ideally they should be fed a meaty diet. Their natural foods are insect larvae and other benthic invertebrates.

The second group is an interesting one and has some hobby representation from time to time. There are five genera in this group: *Andersonia, Belonoglanis, Doumea, Phractura,* and *Trachyglanis*. These catfishes have a long and narrow build and a long, thin caudal peduncle. In varying degrees their bodies display hard and bony armor. This is often on the latter half of the body, but some species have it on the front half as well. In many ways (looks and behavior) these catfishes resemble some of the South American loricariids like *Rineloricaria*. From what's known regarding the diet of these fishes, they predominately feed on insect larvae and other benthic invertebrates. These catfishes will appreciate the same setup as described for *Amphilius*.

Bunocephalus cf. *coracoideus* tend to burrow into the aquarium substrate. Sand is a good choice, although it makes them difficult to see.

Aspredinidae

This small South American family known as banjo catfishes has 37 described species in 13 genera. There's a good amount of variation in size, with the smallest being *Micromyzon akamai*, at only slightly over one-half inch (13 mm) SL, and at the other end of the scale *Aspredo aspredo*, which can reach 15 inches (38 cm) SL. All are found in fresh water with the exception of four (in three genera) that may also be found in brackish or even marine environments. The freshwater species may be found in a wide variety of environments.

Bunocephalus Notes

- *Bunocephalus* have interesting movements, as they aren't real swimmers per se. They crawl along the bottom of their tank. Another way of movement is via jet propulsion. They take in water through their mouths and forcibly expel it through their gill covers. The strength of this is sufficient to propel them forward.
- *Bunocephalus*, like many other catfishes, are capable of producing loud sounds. These occur when the pectoral spines rotate in their sockets.
- *Bunocephalus* get some protection via their cryptic appearance. Also, when they are hassled they will curl the back half of their body around towards the head, forming a circle to semi-circle, no doubt to appear as unappetizing as possible.
- These catfishes shed their skin on a regular basis. The outer layers of skin contain keratin that hardens, and as the fish grows these upper layers must be gotten rid of. They will break up and then slough off as pieces of varying size. During the process the banjos are often seen with grayish skin hanging from parts of their body.

Most banjo cats can be found in areas with many hiding places. This can include mud and sand, in which they will bury themselves as necessary. They're also well known inhabitants of leaf litter, which provides excellent hiding and hunting places for them.

Bunocephalus

For aquarists the most important banjo cats are members of the genus *Bunocephalus,* which contains 9 species, a number of which are imported into the hobby. These species are all quite similar.

Bunocephalus banjos are small. Some species attain a length of close to 5 inches (13 cm) SL, although most do not. They have flattened armored heads that may display various degrees of ridging. The eyes are quite small. The posterior part of the body has rows of small bumpy tubercles running its length. The dorsal fin is small, and there is no adipose fin.

These catfishes aren't good for a busy community setup. Their shyness and slowness make it very easy for other fishes to outcompete them for food. Ideally they should be in a quiet and mellow setup or their own dedicated tank.

A banjo tank's substrate should be of a fine particle size—remember that the banjos like to burrow. Larger banjos can handle standard gravel, but very small ones may find this difficult. If you use a sand substrate, you will most likely see the tank's inhabitants less frequently. They will, of course, come out to eat.

Other tank decor can potentially include some irregular rocks and driftwood for hiding places. You can also create a little fine-leafed plant "forest" for them. Another option is to supply them with a bottom cover of leaves. Boiled dried oak leaves or some of the commercially available almond leaves would be ideal for this. If you did the whole bottom of their tank like this you might not see the banjos very much at all, but some scattered leaves would be a good natural addition to the tank.

Banjos aren't too fussy about water conditions. Feeding banjos also doesn't present any problems. In nature they primarily eat various adult insects (terrestrial and aquatic), insect larvae and nymphs, small worms, some plant matter, and detritus. This latter source is broken-down plant material, which is often rich in microinvertebrates. They also do some scavenging—fish scales and small parts of fish have been found among stomach contents. In captivity they aren't fussy about accepting various flake and other styles of prepared foods. Just remember that banjos have small mouths, so foods should be sized accordingly. Be sure to regularly include at least one prepared food high in vegetal content. Various meaty foods should also be offered daily. Ideal options include bloodworms, tubifex or other small worms, and maybe a bit of brine shrimp.

Pterobunocephalus

Pterobunocephalus is a small genus consisting of two described species. These closely resemble the more flat-headed *Bunocephalus,* and they will grow to around 3½ inches (9 cm) SL. A differentiating characteristic from *Bunocephalus* is the number of rays in the anal fin. It's not overly difficult to count the rays with these slow and inactive catfishes. They can be held up to the aquarium glass and the rays counted using a good magnifying glass. Or a close-up digital photo could be taken. *Bunocephalus* have from five to ten rays in the anal fin; *Pterobunocephalus* have ten to twenty rays.

Pterobunocephalus depressus. The females of this species carry their eggs until they hatch.

This genus has an interesting mode of reproduction, and that's why trying to separate some individuals out from a shipment of *Bunocephalus* would be a worthy task. When these catfish spawn the eggs become attached to the female's underside and are carried around until they hatch. To the best of my knowledge no spawning has taken place in aquaria.

Auchenipteridae

This group of lower Central and South American catfishes is one of my personal favorites. There are currently 95 species in 20 genera. There's a relatively large size variation in the family—*Gelanoglanis nanonocticolus* maxes out around four-fifths of an inch (2 cm) SL, while some *Ageneiosus* species can surpass 2 feet (60 cm) SL. Obviously these larger mid-water swimming *Ageneiosus*—and some other genera such as *Auchenipterus*—don't make good aquarium inhabitants, but there are some smaller species that do.

Auchenipterids are naked catfishes and typically have three pairs of barbels. A noted feature of this family is the various forms of male sexual dimorphism that are linked to the fish's internal fertilization and include: size modified and curved dorsal spines (which can grow quickly during the reproductive phase); elongated and stiffened maxillary (upper jaw) barbels; modified pelvic fins (claspers); and modified anal fins which act as fertilization organs. There are a number of variations with this latter feature. As far as is known, all species are internal fertilizers with the females potentially holding viable male sperm for up to a few months. When their eggs are laid, they are then fertilized. So if you get just one auchenipterid female of any species and it lays eggs, treat them as fertilized eggs just in case.

All auchenipterids are meat eaters and their diet can vary from insects to crustaceans to fishes. This diet is easily replicated and most auchenipterids are not fussy eaters.

Ageneiosus

This genus is composed of ten described species. In the past these fish, along with the genus *Tetranematichthys*, were considered

The Genus *Amaralia*

This somewhat unusual banjo genus currently consists of one described species—*A. hypsiura*. One as yet undescribed species definitely exists, and I wouldn't be surprised if there are more. The maximum size reported is around 5¼ inches (13 cm) SL. *Amaralia* are generally thicker-bodied than *Bunocephalus* and the head and top of the body are ridged in appearance. *Amaralia hypsiura* is very much like the *Bunocephalus* species right down to the shedding of skin.

Amaralia catfishes have been found with the egg clusters of loricariids in their stomachs. No other food sources were observed. However, I have found them very receptive to a wide variety of foods.

Ageneiosus brevis (left) and *A.* cf. *marmoratus* (right) are two species that are suitable for the home aquarium.

as a family-level grouping but they're now generally considered to belong in Auchenipteridae. Some *Ageneiosus*, which are mid-water swimmers, get quite large and aren't good aquarium fishes; these include *A. inermis, A. militaris, A. pardalis, A. polystictus,* and *A. ucayalensis.* But some of the smaller species make interesting aquarium inhabitants—*A. atronasus, A. brevis, A. magoi,* and *A. piperatus.* Most notable among this group is *A. magoi.* This species reaches a full adult size of around 8 inches (20 cm) TL, and sexual dimorphism (and activity) can be seen in 5-inch-TL (13-cm-TL) individuals. *A. magoi* is quite attractive, with a whitish body generously marked with black spots and horizontal lines. Once mature, the males are sexually dimorphic in the shape of the front part of the anal fin, which is used for internal fertilization. When they come into season, other dramatic changes take place. The dorsal spine grows and will at least double in length. It also becomes crooked and develops small bumps/spikes. This morphology of the spine, which will move forward in at least a 45-degree angle, is used for holding the female in place during the mating process. Additionally, the maxillary barbels become hard and elongated and also have hook-like spikes. These barbels can rise straight up and are also used to hold the female in place for mating. This mating process has been observed by a number of aquarists (myself included), but unfortunately fry have yet to be produced.

A. magoi, like other *Ageneiosus,* is a predatory fish, but this doesn't present any problems in captivity. Although they will eat a variety of small fishes, they also eagerly eat most kinds of aquarium foods—bloodworms, krill, and brine shrimp are especially appreciated.

Although hiding places should be provided for *A. magoi,* they are just as likely to lie on the bottom of the tank, often in a group, when not swimming. A small group of them will require a decent-sized tank (at least 50 gallons [200 liters]), but giving them the space will be worth it.

A. magoi. This species will mate in the aquarium, but so far no fry have been produced.

Auchenipterichthys

The most commonly seen auchenipterid in the hobby is the so-called Zamora cat, *Auchenipterichthys coracoideus,* which is imported in large numbers from Peru. It's not overly colorful, but it does present an attractive overall gray-purplish coloration with a neatly arranged series of small white spots. This is a smaller (slightly over 4 inches [10 cm] SL), mostly mid-water group-loving species, so ideally at least four individuals should be purchased together. Look closely at the anal fins when choosing so that you can get males and females. The males show some thickening and slight elongation of the first few rays of the anal fin. There has been at least one report of mid-water spawning activity in this species, with the immediate release of eggs occurring, indicating the possibility that there might be some flexibility in the mode of fertilization with this species. This deserves additional study.

Auchenipterichthys coracoideus. This species does best when kept in small schools of at least four individuals.

Liosomadoras

Both members of this genus are known as jaguar catfishes. *L. oncinus,* the larger of the two at around 8 inches (20 cm) SL, has a true jaguar-like pattern. This species is one of the most beautiful aquarium catfishes, with a base color

ranging from whitish to light brown to an almost golden yellow. The body is richly patterned with dark markings. *L. morrowi*, which reaches around 6 inches (15 cm) SL, is known as the black jaguar. Its base color is gray-brown to blackish; subtle dark markings usually are present.

Upon importation (usually from Brazil), the jaguar cat is often in modestly rough condition and may have a bacterial infection. It's my belief that this is because these fish tend to be a low pH blackwater species and have evolved in waters with low bacterial content. When they're caught and placed in crowded unnatural waters, the resultant stress exposes them to a bacterial attack. Consequently, this is one of the few species that I will regularly use an antibiotic on during quarantine, typically furan-based. This has worked quite well for me, and once the fish have cleared quarantine there are usually no follow-up problems.

Jaguars settle in nicely with a variety of water conditions. Once they're in their regular tank I have found no need to try to keep their water specifically acidic. It should be considered mandatory to provide them with adequate hiding places. Sections of PVC or clay drainage pipes are excellent for this, as is driftwood. If you have more than one jaguar, allow for more diameter room in the pipes, as at times they will crowd together. As with many other auchenipterids, jaguars are more active after lights out. But once they are settled into their new home, many will come out and roam under lighted conditions—especially when food is being served.

Liosomadoras oncinus. The author recommends quarantining the jaguar cat in somewhat acidic water.

Jaguars are good eaters and will take a variety of prepared and meaty foods. In the latter group bloodworms and krill are good choices. Although jaguar cats have rather large mouths, they really don't appear to be fish eaters. But the possibility that they might enjoy a small fish every now and then definitely exists, so choose their tankmates accordingly. Initially, if your jaguars don't come out in the light to feed, just offer their food about a half hour or so after lights out.

Jaguars can be easily sexed by the anal fin modification on the males. Also seen on males is a larger dorsal spine. So far there have been no successful aquarium spawnings that I am aware of, but infertile eggs have been laid, and this is a hopeful sign. Baby jaguars would definitely be a cause for celebration.

"Spotted Tatia"

The genus *Tatia* is a group of small, interesting auchenipterids that are often sold as midnight cats. Notable among this group is the attractive and popular species commonly sold as the "spotted *Tatia.*" This fish isn't a true *Tatia* and currently resides in the genus *Centromochlus*. This appears to be a holding spot—it has been suggested that this fish, *C. perugiae*, and some similar species should actually be placed in their own genus.

This small western Amazonian native reaches a maximum size of around 2½ inches (6 cm) SL. The base color is white and the upper body is covered with darker spots of varying size. Often the arrangement of these spots is presented in a lattice-like pattern.

L. morrowi. Neither of the jaguar cats is known to consume tankmates, but don't put too much trust in either species.

Centromochlus perugiae. Often sold as the spotted tatia, this little catfish is ideal for someone with a smaller tank.

Some of the variation that's seen has raised questions of a closely related species (*C. altae*) also being possibly involved among imports. This is another of those little taxonomic problems needing to be worked out.

This is an ideal catfish for a species tank, and a smaller one at that. Something in the line of 20 gallons (80 liters) would be fine for a group. This species can be sexed easily by examining the anal fin. On females it looks like a regular fin, but on the males the entire fin is bunched and points backwards. For practical purposes it looks very much like the modified anal fin of a male livebearer. Providing a good environment and hiding places will make these catfishes happy. Some really craggy driftwood or sections of PVC pipe would be excellent. Feeding should consist primarily of smaller meaty foods, but just about any standard foods are taken. This species is primarily a surface feeder; in the wild it mainly eats insects that fall into the water. I have used some of the small dried flies that are available for reptiles, and they were greedily eaten. Usually *C. perugiae* individuals stay well hidden when the light's on, but put some food in the tank and they rapidly emerge, eat fast, and return to their hidey holes. At least one feeding a day after lights out is also recommended.

This species has been successfully spawned by a number of aquarists. The large eggs have been found in a pipe along with a female, indicating the possibility of some degree of post-laying parental care. On occasion the eggs will end up out of the tube, and these can be collected and artificially incubated.

Trachelyopterus

There are currently 13 described species assigned to this genus, and a number of them have reached the hobby over the years. Distinguishing between the various species is very difficult, and it's best to use the designation *T.* cf. *galeatus*. The "cf." in this regard means essentially that we are unsure about the exact designation for the fish and that it's best for now to just compare it to the species known to science as *T. galeatus*.

Trachelyopterus are medium-sized catfishes. The largest reaches around 11 inches (28 cm) TL, but most are smaller and range from 6 to 8½ inches (15 to 22 cm) SL. I currently have a nice group of these cats that were collected in Peru. During the day the fish hide in their pipes and caves, but the addition of a favorite food to the tank brings them out in no time. As soon as the food is consumed it's back to the hidey-holes. At night they're out cruising and interacting. There has been at least one successful spawning of a member of this genus. The eggs, like those of many other auchenipterids, develop a surrounding clear envelope that makes them become quite large after they're released into the water. This is definitely another genus/species to work with towards additional captive reproduction.

Bagridae

With the transferring of most of the African "bagrids" to the family Claroteidae, this family became predominately Asian in its distribution. There's one African genus in Bagridae—*Bagrus* with nine species—but these are generally large food fishes without much aquarium potential. The Asian representatives of this family are placed in around 18 genera which contain approximately 200 species. Some of these, such as *Sperata* and *Rita* spp., attain very large sizes, but there are numerous species that are good candidates for aquaria.

These fish have a reasonably developed adipose fin and four pairs of barbels. All bagrids are primarily meat eaters. There are more than a few species that feed heavily on other fishes, but most of the good aquarium candidates typically feed on invertebrates.

Bagrichthys macracanthus. The black lancer needs both a lot of swimming space and several hiding spots.

Bagrichthys

This genus is composed of the lancer cats, a name based on the

Mystus carcio or *M. tengara*? Problems with identification of the striped *Mystus* are still to be worked out.

generally long and high dorsal fin that's seen on mature individuals. There are seven species, and a number of them are imported. The most common is *B. macracanthus*, the black lancer. This species typically has a solid jet black base color. Even the fins, except for the caudal, which is clear, are blackish in color. Along the midline is a thin horizontal white line that goes from behind the head to the caudal peduncle. The black lancer reaches a maximum size of around 9 inches (23 cm) SL.

Maintaining the black lancer presents no special problems as long as there are ample tank space and hiding places. Initially lancers will hide, but once they're settled in they will become a bit more visible. Having some mid-water dither fishes present can help them feel more comfortable. This all speaks to having a single lancer. If there are more than one present, things most likely will be a bit more interesting. Males will chase females, but as long as there's enough swimming space and hiding areas this is usually not serious. But male-on-male aggression can be rough, and it's often very difficult to keep two males in the same tank. Once they start to mature these catfish are easy to sex. Males have an elongated whitish genital papilla (the small tube that releases sperm) in front of the anal fin. This hangs down and is slightly aimed towards the rear. Also, the nasal barbels of males are at least twice the length of those of females.

Lancers are very catholic in their dietary preferences and eagerly eat a wide variety of prepared and meaty foods.

There are no reports of captive breeding among the *Bagrichthys* species. This would suggest a worthy project for interested aquarist.

Hemibagrus

This is a large genus (32 species) which contains a number of larger predators. Somewhat smaller species that would probably make interesting aquarium inhabitants haven't yet made an appearance in the hobby.

Two species have been regulars for some time—*H. wyckioides*, slightly over 3 feet (1 m) SL, and *H. wyckii*, around 28 inches (71 cm) SL. The first species, which is gray-bodied, with a red caudal fin, is known as the Asian red-tailed cat. The second, which has a black body and a white trim on the upper caudal lobe, is called the crystal eye cat based on the reflective quality of the eyes. Both species are similar in a number of ways. They are predatory; if they can't eat another fish they are likely to just beat it to death. I have had both species, and they both ended up living solitary lives. In living such a life they often take to rearranging the tank. They dig relentlessly. I have also watched my (former) Asian red tail spend a good part of one day destroying a fairly sturdy box filter. This was in a heated fish room, so I didn't have to worry about an in-tank submersible heater, which they're also reported to attack. Such devices would need protection! You will also need secured tops for their tanks. My 16-inch (41-cm) red tail unfortunately perished by leaping out of its tank—which was covered with a plastic top weighed down with a couple of pounds of shale.

These critters no longer hold any allure for me. You should be really sure that you know what you're getting into with these catfishes. Think about it.

Mystus

This genus of 30 species is a catch-all of sorts. No doubt some of the included species will at some future date be assigned to different or new genera. In any case, a number of them are available in varying degrees.

M. bimaculatus: This Sumatran species has been in the hobby for a long time and is commonly sold as the two-spot *Mystus* or the clown catfish. This is a small species that reaches a bit over 2½ inches (6 cm) SL. When the fish are happy the base color is a pleasant maroon and the two spots are dark round blotches on the shoulder; with a dark band-like mark on the caudal peduncle. They are fairly social and do nicely in groups.

Mystus bocourti (top) and *Mystus leucophasis* (bottom) are easy-to-keep catfish, allowing for their size. *M. leucophasis* swims upside down at all times.

Mystus tengara is one of the striped species in which there is some contention in regards to its proper name.

If you like plants, so will these catfish, and the plants will be used as additional cover. The same low-pH bacterial infection situation that affects jaguar cats also affects this species. But beyond this, these attractive little bagrids offer no particular problems. They are active and attractive, and they feast on just about any foods that you care to offer.

M. bocourti: This dramatic-looking species matches the black lancer in having an extremely elongated dorsal fin, but it is easily distinguished by its body form and silvery-gray coloration. It's also available in a very attractive commercially produced albino form. *M. bocourti* reaches a maximum length of around 9½ inches (24 cm) SL, but it has a well-developed caudal fin with an elongated upper lobe, and this will easily add another 2 inches (5 cm) or so to the total length. You can set up this fish similar to what you provide for *M. bimaculatus,* keeping in mind that some open swimming space, in addition to hiding areas, will be needed. Feeding is not a problem—standard and meaty fare is ideal.

M. leucophasis: For many years this was a, if not the, mystical Asian catfish. Now it's commercially bred and commonplace. It's still a magnificent catfish. This is truly an upside-down catfish, much more so than any *Synodontis* I'm aware of. I've kept *M. leucophasis* for many years and have yet to see one in a belly-down position for more than a rare second. As an adult it's totally black and its sides are sprinkled with small silvery to pinkish reflective spots. This is a highly territorial fish; it'll take over a cave and defend it against all comers. Tube-like structures seem to be preferred—I regularly use either PVC or clay drainage pipes. Tankmates, even if tougher, should also be chosen by size, as this species will eat smaller fishes. Since it can max out at close to 1 foot (30 cm), this rules out more than a few possible tankmates. There are practically no meaty foods that this species will not eat with gusto.

"Striped Mystus": This is basically a catch-all grouping of *Mystus* catfishes that can be quite difficult to differentiate. In general, commercial imports may be sold under a number of names including *M. tengara* and *M. vittatus*. I have even seen groups them being sold as 4-line pims. *Mystus* can quickly be distinguished from *Pimelodus* species by the

Corydoras britskii was part of the genus *Brochis* until recently.

presence of their nasal barbels. They range from around 3 inches (8 cm) SL to well over 1 foot (30 cm) SL. Keep this in mind and plan accordingly. The care and feeding of each of these species is the same, so no particular problems should be encountered with them.

Pseudomystus

We touched on this genus earlier in the chapter—the Asian bumblebee cats—so be sure that they aren't confused with the smaller *Akysis* species when considering a possible purchase, as individuals from both genera go by the same common name.

There are about 18 species in this genus; the most commonly seen is *P. siamensis,* from Thailand. *P. siamensis* has a dark body with three (sometimes four) lighter bands that encircle the upper body. The caudal fin is clear and has a dark blotch (or blotches) in each lobe.

This species doesn't get very large (about 6 inches [15 cm] SL), so it has good aquarium potential, but can be territorial and scrappy. If there's more than one *P. siamensis* in a tank, be sure to have hiding places widely separated.

There are no feeding problems that will be encountered, other than that any small fishes in the tank will be possibly eaten, especially at night.

Callichthyidae

Whether this family name is recognized or not there can hardly be a freshwater aquarist who hasn't kept a catfish belonging to it. Such is the power of the (sometimes considered lowly) *Corydoras* catfish. They are far from lowly and over the years have been elevated from being just necessary scavengers to the rank of exciting and highly desirable catfishes.

This family of Central and South American armored catfishes ranges from Panama to Argentina and is composed of around 195 species in eight or nine genera. Of this group about 150 species belong to the genus *Corydoras*. And on top of this there are numerous undiagnosed species that currently have only a C-number designation.

There are two subfamilies in Callichthyidae—Corydoradinae and Callichthyinae. Corydoradinae consists of three genera: *Corydoras, Scleromystax,* and *Aspidoras*. Species of the first genus are widely available in the hobby and are a great success story, especially as it relates to captive reproduction. It seems that there's hardly a *Corydoras* species that cannot be eventually coaxed to spawn in captivity. There's a growing legion of *Corydoras* specialists who are having amazing successes with this group.

Scleromystax is composed of four species. The most popular and widely known of these is the magnificent *S. barbatus*. But contention about *S. barbatus* exists. There's a group that maintains that the Sao Paulo version of this species, which was named *S. kronei*, is a valid species. Ferraris places *S. kronei* as a synonym of *S. barbatus*.

Most of the *Scleromystax* are southern Brazilian coastal forest species, a number of which are experiencing greatly declining populations. At least one species, *S. macropterus*, is officially listed as endangered in Brazil. A strong need for a steady source of aquarium-raised stock is imperative.

Aspidoras (20 species) is less commonly seen in the hobby. So there's also the importance here of trying to maintain, spawn, and get those *Aspidoras* species into the hobby as they might become available as a result of breeding efforts. Most commonly seen as of late is *A. pauciradiatus*, a small species (a bit over 1 inch [2.5 cm] SL for a large female) that has never become firmly established in the hobby.

The second subfamily, Callichthyinae, is like a whole different group of catfishes, even though anatomically

C-Numbers

With the success of the L-Number system under its belt, in 1993 the German magazine *DATZ* started a similar project for *Corydoras* and their close relatives. Exactly as with the L-Numbers, photos of catfishes with assigned C-Numbers were published in the magazine. As with the L-Number system, many of the fishes with C-Numbers have been subsequently identified or described as new. But many others are still just a C-Number whose value is in providing a common language with which to discuss them.

A gallery of *Corydoras*: (top left down) *C. aeneus, C. haraldschultzi, C. metae, C. panda C. nattereri*, and *C. habrosus*.

There is more to the family Callichthyidae than the cories. Some fine aquarium denizens include *Callichthys callichthys* (top), *Dianema urostriatum* (center left), *Hoplosternum littorale* (center right), *Lepthoplosternum pectorale* (bottom right), and *Megalechis thoracata* (bottom left) among others.

they're bound together with the previous genera. While the Corydoradinae place their eggs and give them no further parental care, this subfamily, as far as known, is tied together by the reproductive method of the males' building and tending of bubblenests, which hold the eggs and developing fry. The genera in this group are: *Callichthys* (four species); *Dianema* (porthole cats, two species); *Hoplosternum* (three species); *Lepthoplosternum* (dwarf hoplo cats, six species); and *Megalechis* (two species). Some of these interesting catfishes were once aquarium favorites but have decreased in popularity. It's fine to go with the *Corydoras* and their close relatives, but consider giving some tank space to their larger and more reproductively interesting cousins.

Chacidae

Writing about *Chaca chaca* in 1823, Hamilton-Buchanan used a line that I never tire of reading: "Of all the horrid animals of this tribe the *chaca* of this district is the most disagreeable to behold…all persons turn away from it with loathing." Now that's a description that really makes you want to run out and buy some of these fish for your aquarium!

This is a small Asian family, commonly known as frogmouth catfishes, consisting of three species in the genus *Chaca*—*C. bankanensis* (from peninsular Malaysia, southeastern Thailand, and widespread in Indonesia-Sumatra, western Borneo); *C. burmensis* (Myanmar—Irrawaddy and Sittang River basins); and *C. chaca* (northwestern India, Bangladesh). *C. bankanensis* and *C. chaca* are seen more in the hobby than *C. burmensis*. The possibility of importation of *C. burmensis* has been raised, but I'm not aware of any that have made it into the U.S. hobby. If you can get a definite country of origin locality

Chaca chaca (left) and *C. bankanensis* (right). These strange catfish may do best when kept by themselves.

Auchenoglanis occidentalis. Although a peaceable fish, the giraffe catfish grows to an enormous size, so it is a poor choice for the average aquarist.

for any *Chaca* that you might run across, this will tell which species is involved, though such information is admittedly often difficult to obtain.

The coloration of the two available species can run from tan to dark brown to blackish, and it's not uncommon for all of these colors to be mixed on one individual. Mottled patterns are also not uncommon. Typically, *C. chaca* tends to be lighter in coloration, but this is far from being a hard rule. The general shape of *Chaca* cats is quite distinctive. On close examination the sides of the head can be seen to have numerous little flaps of skin or cirri (hair-like projections). The skin on the body usually has similar appendages or little granular bumps. *Chaca* are known to reach a maximum length of a little over 9 inches (23 cm) SL. *C. chaca* has been spawned in captivity.

Aquarium care of *Chaca* species isn't overly difficult. They don't need a deep tank—something in the line of a 20-gallon (80-liter) long or 30-gallon (120-liter) tank will be fine. Like most other catfishes, they can get along within a good range of temperature and pH values. The frogmouths like to dig, so a finer substrate is suggested. You could also use leaves, such as dried and then lightly boiled oak or almond leaves, to provide cover. Such leaves tend to lower the pH; this would probably be beneficial, especially for *C. bankanensis,* which typically lives in blackwater forest streams with naturally lower pH values. The distribution of *C. chaca* tends to be mostly outside forested areas.

Although the *Chaca* species make fascinating aquarium inhabitants, they are without question suited more for the specialist interested in a single-specimen tank. *Chaca* are highly predatory cats not meant for a community situation. Their natural diet consists of smaller fishes and shrimps. Other living meaty items like worms are also no doubt consumed. They aren't real chasers of their prey, but have more of a lurk-and-gulp style of feeding. It's also reported that they'll use their short maxillary barbels to mimic the appearance of a wriggling worm to attract prey. Once the prey is close, the huge mouth is quickly thrown open, creating a suction that pulls the victim inside. Some *Chaca* might be tempted with nonliving meaty foods, but this is far from a sure bet and you'll have to offer them a regular diet of small live fishes. Be sure to gutload these feeder fishes with a good-quality dry food before offering them to the *Chaca*. (See Chapter 2.) *Chaca* are thought to be poisonous by locals, and there have been some suggestion by aquarists that this might be true. There is a report of feeder guppies dying after they were observed nibbling on the skin of *C. bankanensis*. This is certainly something to keep in mind. It has also been suggested that *Chaca* may exude a skin secretion that will kill other fishes in their tank.

Claroteidae

The family Claroteidae is composed of what used to be the African bagrids, minus the genus *Bagrus*. This family comprises 84 species among 17 genera. The largest and most widespread is *Chrysichthys* (44 species). Many claroteids can get quite large, and most are used as food fishes. All have a relatively smooth body with either three or four pairs of barbels. Members of the family range widely in size. At the upper end are catfishes that can reach nearly 4 feet (1.2 m) TL, and on the other end of the scale is *Lophiobagrus asperispinis*, which reaches only around 1 inches (3.4 cm) TL. All members of the family are basically carnivorous, but varying degrees of plant material/detritus may also be eaten, at least on a seasonal basis. The meaty part of the diet in many species is composed mainly of insects, crustaceans, etc., but many others are confirmed fish eaters. All in all, any member of this family should be considered as a potential eater of smaller fishes, and tankmates should be chosen accordingly.

Auchenoglanis occidentalis

Commonly called the giraffe catfish, this species is one of the so-called gentle giants, and the word "giant" shouldn't be taken lightly. The young are attractively patterned and make for a nice aquarium species. They're relatively mild mannered and are constantly sifting through the gravel searching for leftovers. But they grow very large and will strain the confines of a home aquarium. They can reach around 3½ feet (1 m) TL.

While most *Chrysichthys* species tend to be patternless there are some exceptions.

Chrysichthys ornatus. While not difficult to keep, this catfish needs some live fishes in its diet.

Chrysichthys

Most aquarists are introduced to *Chrysichthys* species via the so-called aluminum catfishes from West Africa. They usually have a silvery to silvery gray/brown body color with little or no patterning. A few different species might show up in shipments, but *C. nigrodigitatus* appears to be the most common. *C. walkeri* and *C. auratus* are two other species that might also be encountered. *C. walkeri* reaches around 8 inches (20 cm) SL and is the smallest of the three. *C. auratus* can reach up to almost 14 inches (36 cm) SL. *C. nigrodigitatus* is the giant of this group at around 26 inches (66 cm) SL. Attempting to identify young *Chrysichthys* is problematic, so just be prepared for potentially large catfishes should you try any of these species.

Other than the potential sizes, these catfishes shouldn't be any trouble. *Chrysichthys* aren't fussy eaters and will eagerly take a wide variety of prepared and meaty foods. Smaller fishes are a natural food for these species, so be sure that tankmates are appropriate. Water conditions aren't a problem; a wide range of normal tropical conditions is acceptable as long as good water quality is maintained.

C. ornatus: This is arguably the most attractive species of the genus. The base coloration is yellowish (sometimes almost golden) to tan, and there are dark brown to black markings on the head and body. Each lobe of the caudal fin has a dark elongated-band-type marking. In many ways the coloration of this fish is very close to that of *Goeldiella eques*—the two have been confused in some hobby literature. (*G. eques* has very long maxillary barbels; *C. ornatus* has short ones.) *C. ornatus* isn't an overly large species—it reaches around 10 inches (25 cm) SL. They aren't fussy at all when it comes to food, but ideally they should be fed a good amount of meaty foods, including small live fishes. They're highly predatory in nature, so tankmates must be chosen with care. Don't underestimate this cat's ability to eat other fishes—they are quite proficient at it.

Lake Tanganyikan Claroteids

Africa's Lake Tanganyika has fascinating fish fauna, and the claroteids from there are no exception. But before moving on, a brief word is needed. Lake Tanganyika is well known for its high pH values, which can range from 8.6 to slightly over 9.0. Maintaining freshwater aquaria at such pH values carries a potentially serious problem in that ammonia becomes increasingly toxic at higher pH values. Fortunately, the various catfishes of Lake Tanganyika adapt well to lower values and will thrive and reproduce at them. I generally recommend trying to maintain such fishes at a pH around 7.0 to 7.6 or so. There are commercial buffers available, or you can place some dolomite into either your power filter or a separate internal box filter to help maintain the slightly higher values.

Chrysichthys (Bathybagrus) sianenna: Lake Tanganyika has its own little flock of seven *Chrysichthys* species (most of these species are considered to be in the genus *Bathybagrus* by some authorities). Most get rather large, but *C. sianenna* is a smaller species that's imported from time to time. This catfish reaches a maximum size of a touch over 9 inches (23 cm) SL. *C. sianenna* is an interesting aquarium species, but as with all *Chrysichthys,* make sure that it isn't placed with small fishes.

Lophiobagrus: Lophiobagrus contains four species. At least two, *L. brevispinis* and *L. cyclurus,* are imported into the hobby. The other two species, *L. aquilus* and *L. asperispinis*, might have been imported, but I'm unaware of any confirmation regarding this. *Lophiobagrus* are all small fishes that are ideal for the aquarium. The maximum known size is just a little over 3 inches (8 cm) SL for *L. cyclurus. L. brevispinis* is smaller at just a bit over 2 inches SL (5 cm). *Lophiobagrus* strongly resemble the young of American bullheads (genus *Ameiurus*) right down to the presence of nasal barbels. They have subtle coloration, grayish to dark brownish-

Lophiobagrus brevispinis. This species and the others in the genus appreciate rock piles and caves in their tanks.

Oxydoras niger. Occasionally available as a small juvenile, this talking catfish can grow over 4 feet (1.2 m) in length.

black, but when happy they often display a purplish cast. *L. cyclurus* and *L. brevispinis* are similar, but one color difference is that *L. cyclurus* has a thin clear area at the end of the caudal fin while *C. brevispinis* does not. In addition, the caudal fin of *L. cyclurus* is slightly rounded while that of *L. brevispinis* is reported to be "truncate to scarcely rounded."

All *Lophiobagrus* are from rocky areas, so the tank should be set up accordingly. Piles of rocks can be built, with open space between them, to allow the fish to establish territories. Broken flower pot crockery can also be used to good effect.

Lophiobagrus offers no problems when it comes to feeding, and they will take a wide variety of prepared and meaty foods.

There has been captive breeding with this genus. Male mouthbrooding has been observed in two species in the wild, but aquarium reports are at times contradictory. This is an ideal area for additional research by aquarists.

Phyllonemus: The genus *Phyllonemus*, which currently consists of three species (*P. brichardi, P. filinemus,* and *P. typus*) is surely one of the neatest groups of aquarium claroteids. The most commonly seen species is *P. typus*. What appears to possibly be *P. filinemus* may be seen on very rare occasion, and I'm unaware of any imports of *P. brichardi*.

P. typus is an ideal aquarium catfish and reaches a maximum length of around 3½ inches (9 cm) SL. The upper body color is a pleasant reddish-brown, and the abdomen is white. The most noticeable feature of this species is the long maxillary barbels, which terminate in flat black wide tips. The other two species have more standard barbels that don't show extreme widenings at the tips. There may be changes coming in identifying members of this genus—at least five new species are awaiting formal description. What's so fascinating about this species (and *P. filinemus* for sure and probably also *P. brichardi*) is that it's a pair-bonding bi-parental mouthbrooder and that there already have been a number of reported captive spawnings. I experienced some pair formation in a group of *P. typus*, but unfortunately due to circumstances beyond my control had to pass the fish along to a friend, who subsequently did get some successful spawning activity. If you wish to work with this species, obtain a group of at least a half dozen and set them up by themselves in a tank as described above for *Lophiobagrus*.

Doradidae

This family is composed of the so-called talking catfishes, a name based on the sounds they can produce by rotating their pectoral spines in their sockets and by manipulation of their swim bladders. This vocalization is by no means unique to this family but the talking cats name has stuck for them. In other sources they are also called thorny catfishes, and this might be a more fitting descriptive name. Members of this family are widespread in South America. There are approximately 78 described species placed in 31 genera. More new species descriptions are currently in the works, as well as some juggling of species among genera, so there will be more changes to come within this family.

The range of sizes in this family's is quite extreme. At the low end there's the genus *Physopyxis,* which has a maximum size of less than 1½ inches (4 cm) SL, and then there's *Oxydoras niger,* which has recorded lengths of over 48 inches (1.2 m) SL. One other doradid, *Lithodoras dorsalis,* comes in a close second at around 40 inches (1 m) TL.

Doradids are tough-skinned catfishes characterized by the presence of mid-line scutes (bony external plates or shells) armed with a backward-pointing sharp spine. In some species these spines can be quite large. In others only a few spines may be present, but for the most part they tend to run the length of the body. Regardless of the species, they deserve attention. First, they can potentially cause severe cuts to the hands of an unsuspecting or careless hobbyist. Second, like the well-developed dorsal and pectoral spines, these scute spines can easily become entangled in a loose-weave net.

Agamyxis pectinifrons. This species prefers tight-fitting hiding places it can wedge itself into.

Doradids can be broken down into two large groups based on the morphology of the maxillary barbels—one group has barbels that are simple and lack any branching, while representatives of the second group have (sometimes quite noticeable) branches on these barbels. Many doradids are at least partially social and will hide together during the day. Others, such as the "Sierra cat" group, live in large schools; many times up to four or five species may be found schooling together. As aquarium catfishes the doradids are for the most part excellent. Only the very large size of some species presents potential problems.

Agamyxis pectinifrons

This is one of the so-called raphael catfishes. This species, which presents a black body with numerous white to yellow spots, is commonly called the spotted raphael. Although it has a smaller adult size (around 6 inches [15 cm] SL) than both the striped and longnose raphael catfishes (both of which will be covered shortly later in this chapter), all else in regard to the captive maintenance of *A. pectinifrons* can be considered comparable.

Megalodoras uranoscopus

I've tended to speak against having most larger catfishes as aquarium inhabitants, but there's always a bit of wiggle room as long as the aquarist goes the proverbial extra mile when it comes to providing adequate tank space. This species is one that I tend to make an

Megalodoras uranoscopus. Other than problems associated with its adult size, this is not a difficult species to keep.

exception for. *M. uranoscopus*, which may be seen as *M. irwini* in older literature, is at any size a distinctive and attractive species. The base coloration is black, and the body (especially the plates on which the side spines are located) has large yellowish to whitish areas of color. This species can reach around 21 inches (53 cm) SL. To adequately house a catfish of this size you should consider at least a 6-foot-long (1.8-m-long) tank. The width should also be considered—wider is better than narrower. In standard 6-foot tanks this would mean a 180-gallon (720-liter) tank, which is 2 feet (60 cm) wide, as opposed to a 125- or 150-gallon (500- or 600-liter) tank, both of which are only 18 inches (46 cm) wide. Other than its tank's size this species presents no real problems.

Two Large Doradids

Two very large doradids show up as young individuals among imports: *Pterodoras granulosus* and *Oxydoras niger*. I have seen both of these sold under the name "prehistoric cat." While they are fascinating when young, what are you going to do with catfishes that may eventually reach adult sizes of 28 inches (71 cm) SL and 40 inches (1 m) SL, respectively? Although these are generally peaceful and unproblematic catfishes, they just get too big for most home aquaria. Avoid them.

Orinocodoras eigenmanni

This is an attractive doradid that isn't imported under its own name. It's inevitably found mixed in among shipments of the striped raphael. The common name for this species is longnose raphael—this is the tipoff on how it can be identified. The striped raphael has a rounded head ("nose"), while that of *Orinocodoras* is noticeably more pointed. This can be observed from both the top and the side. The longnosed raphael is a very nice catfish, and its care (social conditions, tank conditions, diet, etc.) is in every way comparable with that of the striped raphael. Sizewise this species is similar, reaching a maximum size of around 8 inches (20 cm) SL. As with many other (but not all) catfishes, the females usually attain the larger size.

Platydoras cf. armatulus

This name is being used for the standard striped raphael. The overall taxonomy of the genus *Platydoras* is complicated. The typically used scientific name for this fish is *P. costatus*. However, it now appears that the distribution of *P. costatus* is limited to French Guiana and Suriname. In any case, it doesn't have the wide white to yellowish mid-line band associated with the available hobby species (Mark Sabaj Perez, personal communication).

Orinocodoras eigenmanni. This nice aquarium fish is usually mislabeled and found among groups of striped raphaels (*Playdoras*).

The striped raphael is a great aquarium fish and can be successfully maintained in a wide variety of situations. It will fit nicely into most community situations, but it would also be interesting to set up a species-type tank. It isn't a schooling species but will generally get along with its own kind. Just be sure to provide plenty of caves, pipes, or other hiding areas. If keeping a few together there might be disputes over such places, but this is usually not a major problem. Although striped raphaels will regularly be more active under low-light conditions, once they're acclimated to tank life they'll tend to come out rather quickly at any time favorite foods are offered. The striped raphael can reach up to around 9 inches (23 cm) SL. *Platydoras* tend to be omnivores/invertivores in nature and will eat just about any commercial food you offer.

"Sierra" Cats

Sold under this common name (and also as "mouse cats") are a generally similar group of interesting doradids. In all, six genera are involved: *Doras, Hassar, Hemidoras, Leptodoras, Nemadoras,* and *Opsodoras.* All are more or less similar in having a silvery-gray base body coloration. Many may also show some degree of black coloration in their dorsal fins. Another feature that helps to combine them is that all have branched maxillary barbels. This isn't unique to this group, but outside of them it's rare. The mentioned genera show variance in their nose shape, with some being elongate while others are rounded. There's some general taxonomic confusion with this group, but work is underway to help straighten this out.

From an aquarium maintenance point of view these catfishes are all similar. They are all schooling species, so when purchasing some it'd be a good idea to pick up three or

Platydoras cf. *armatulus*. The striped raphael is easy to keep and does well in most community setups.

four individuals. In nature they tend to live around sandy areas in flowing water, and as far as is known they all feed on various small invertebrates. In aquaria they aren't fussy eaters and will take just about all standard prepared and meaty foods. It's good to provide some current for them and good biological filtration. A program of increased water changes will also be beneficial.

Heptapteridae

This Central and South American family consists of 24 genera containing 189 species. Before the erection of this family, at least one genus of the catfishes (*Pimelodella*) was considered as very typical pimelodid. Heptapteridae, along with Pimelodidae and Pseudopimelodidae, once made up the family Pimelodidae. Some authorities still maintain the use of only one family. Heptapterids are generally small to medium-sized catfishes; more than 60 percent of the

Brachyrhamdia imitator. The resemblance of this species to the cory cats is striking. Occasionally it will be found mixed in with cories.

included species don't exceed 4 inches (10 cm) SL. The maximal size in the family is around 15 inches (38 cm) SL, but this is uncommon. Heptapterids tend to be elongated, sometimes extremely so. There are three pairs of barbels—one maxillary, which can be quite long on some species, and two mandibular.

The species that come into the hobby are easy to care for. Beyond providing them good-quality water and a varied nutritious diet there are no major concerns. All of these fishes predominately feed on insects and their larvae and various other invertebrates, but some of the larger forms are known to regularly consume small fishes.

Brachyrhamdia

This genus contains five species, the most common of which is *B. imitator*. The species name refers to the fish's color pattern, which resembles that of certain *Corydoras* species. *B. imitator* has a base color of light brown to tan with numerous small dark spots scattered on the body. A dark mask runs vertically through the eyes. There's also a similar but wider band that starts in the front part of the dorsal fin and runs about halfway down the body. Although the species is sometimes imported under its own name, it's also possible to find individuals mixed in among some *Corydoras* imports. Although the pattern may be similar, the naked body and the long maxillary barbels of *Brachyrhamdia* are a quick giveaway. *B. imitator* reaches only around 3 inches (8 cm) SL. Usually the largest individuals turn out to be females. These are a great schooling fish, so try to get a group if you can. They're invertebrate feeders but will accept just about any commercial food.

Pimelodella sp. Most species in the genus have a black stripe from nose to tail.

Goeldiella eques

I have favorites in each group of catfishes that I've kept, and among the heptapterids this is a favorite. This moderately larger heptapterid reaches a maximum length of around 12 inches (30 cm) SL. It's attractively patterned with a tan to yellowish base color. The front part of the dorsal fin is black, and as the fin reaches the body it angles forward, creating the look of

Rhamdia quelen. This is a large, aggressive catfish best left to experienced aquarists.

a horse bridle, hence the specific epithet of *eques*. A dark line runs partially lengthwise down the top of the body beneath the dorsal fin and part of the long and well-developed adipose fin. *G. eques* might get mixed up with another species (*Chrysichthys ornatus*) from time to time. The overall color/pattern is somewhat similar, but *Goeldiella* can be easily identified by its long maxillary barbels (short in *C. ornatus*), as mentioned earlier.

G. eques is a catfish that should have a good amount of room, even when smaller. Be sure to also provide cover to make it comfortable. I have caught some of these (in Brazil) hiding out in pieces of wood during the day, so driftwood would be an ideal and natural choice. Although various aquatic invertebrates are eaten in the wild, fish make up a large part of the diet of this species—both other catfishes and characoids are known to be eaten. Ideally it's good to provide some gutloaded live feeder fishes. Keep this in mind when choosing tankmates—and don't underestimate the capacity of this attractive species to eat other fishes.

Pimelodella

This is the largest genus in the family and includes 71 described species found from Costa Rica to Argentina. Most are similar in appearance and generally show a yellowish to tan base color. In most—but not all—species there's a dark narrow band that runs the length of the body from the nose to the caudal fin. This band is only interrupted by the eyes and partially by the operculum. These elongated, long-barbeled catfishes are standard imports and are typically sold as *Pimelodella* sp. or sometimes as *P. gracilis*. This last name is valid, but its attachment to any imported species should be considered tentative at best. Although many species tend to stay on the smaller side (under 6 inches [15 cm] TL), there are also some large forms (at least 14 inches [36 cm] SL), but generally you will get one of the smaller ones. All *Pimelodella* are, as far as is known, schooling species, so be sure to pick out at least three and provide them with adequate open tank space, as they do like to cruise around. *Pimelodella* have fairly small dorsal and pectoral spines, but they can pack a nasty sting. These fins can also be a problem in getting tangled up in nets having a large weave size.

Rhamdia

This genus has a very large distribution; its 17 species can be found from Mexico to Argentina. The species most likely to be encountered is *R. quelen,* which is found throughout the genus's range. *R. quelen* is rarely sold under its own name. The best that you might hope for is seeing it as *"Rhamdia* sp." I've seen it sold under a number of common names, including just as *"Pimelodella."* My favorite common name, which I saw a few years ago, is sewer cat. This name certainly has some validity in that *Rhamdia* (and quite a few other fishes, including some cichlids) found around human habitations are known to feed on human feces.

   R. quelen is an elongate catfish. The adipose fin is usually quite long and has its origin close to the dorsal fin. As with all other heptapterids, there are three pairs of barbels, of which the maxillary pair is quite long. As you might imagine, a catfish from such a large range can be quite variable in color and pattern, but even at their best *Rhamdia* colors can only be described as subtle.

Horabagrus brachysoma. Although endangered in nature, *H. brachysoma* is bred for the commercial trade.

The overall coloration tends towards grayish-brown, often with a scattering of smaller and darker spots. In some individuals a dark mid-line band can be present. This active species reaches a bit over 15 inches (38 cm) SL, so adequate room is required. *Rhamdia* can often be tough on conspecifics—be sure to provide adequate hiding places should you have more than one specimen. Tankmates must be chosen carefully, because *Rhamdia* will eat small fishes. They also eat a wide variety of foods. You shouldn't have trouble feeding them; just about everything will be accepted. Because of their temperaments and potential sizes, I feel *Rhamdia* cats should be tackled only after you've had some experience in the hobby.

Horabagridae

This small family of Asian catfishes, which was not accepted as such by Ferraris, was formally proposed in 2005. It was erected based on the two Indian species—*Horabagrus brachysoma* and *H. nigricollaris*. Two non-Indian schilbeid genera, *Platytropius* and *Pseudeutropius,* were also included in the family. *H. brachysoma* is common in the hobby, *H. nigricollaris* a little less so. There are also at least two species of *Pseudeutropius* (*P. brachypopterus* and *P. moolenburghae*) that have off-and-on availability. These species are noticeably different from *Horabagrus* and have more of a similarity to glass catfish. These social, grouping species are also interesting in that they often swim with their barbels pointing forward. Both species are around 4 inches (10 cm) SL and can be maintained as with the Asian glass cat, *Kryptopterus minor*. As aquarium catfishes the two *Horabagrus* species present no special problems. They accept a reasonable variety of water conditions as long as good biological filtration and regular water changes are provided.

H. brachysoma

H. brachysoma is native to southern India, has a fairly restricted distribution, and is considered an endangered species. The reasons for this status appear to be man-made and include alteration and pollution of the natural habitat and overfishing (for human food). But this species is commercially bred for the aquarium hobby, so wild populations are not affected. Such breeding takes place in Thailand and India, and in the past at least some Florida fish farms were successfully working with this species.

US–Native Catfishes

The family Ictaluridae currently consists of 64 species in seven genera. For the aquarium, you may be able to keep bullheads (*Ameriurus* spp.), especially some of the smaller forms (and this is relative), such as the so-called snail bullheads. All of them come in at under 1 foot (30 cm) TL. Most other bullheads top out at between 1½ and 2 feet (46 to 60 cm) TL. The best North American catfishes for the aquarium are the smaller madtoms (*Noturus* spp.) from east of the Rockies. Most of these range from 4 to 6 inches (10 to 15 cm) TL, but there are some larger (*N. flavus*, up to slightly over 1 foot TL) and some smaller (*N. stanauli*, about 1½ inches [4 cm]) madtoms. I have personally kept two species of madtoms (*N. flavus* and *N. gyrinus*) and found them to be fascinating.

But there's a caveat. Of the approximately 34 species, or undescribed populations of madtoms, at least 14 have a conservation status ranging from vulnerable to possibly extinct. There are also additional populations that will no doubt represent new species, and some of these will also end up deserving conservation status. We think of catfishes of special concern elsewhere but often forget to think about the situation in our own back yard. The various U.S. states and the federal government have laws relating to fresh waters and the fishes therein. These may be general coverage laws, but there are also numerous special protection laws—some might relate specifically to madtoms. It's best to not go headlong into local waters looking for catfishes, or any other fishes for that matter. It is all too possible that you will be breaking the law. If you have any interest in native fishes, check out the North American Native Fishes Association (www.nanfa.org). With that source you can make local contacts and generally find out whatever you might want to know about fishes in your area, or elsewhere, which species are legal to collect, and what might be required to collect some of them. It's a topflight organization and a prime gateway to North American aquarium fishes.

Noturus insignis, the margined madtom.

This species is an attractive mid-water catfish with a usually yellowish base color, but sometimes some nice greenish coloration can also be seen. Larger fish also develop an attractive red coloration on the caudal fin. Behind the head, at mid-line, is a black shoulder spot surrounded by a goldish yellow trim. It's a pleasure to get young fish and watch them grow, because the colors improve as they do. The maximum size is listed at slightly less than 18 inches (46 cm) SL. The sun cat is fairly social with its own kind, so it's ideal to have at least two or three of them.

Many of the plecos breed well in the aquarium, and some color varieties are available. Shown here are a normal and an albino sailfin pleco, *Pterygoplichthys gibbiceps.*

The sun cat is mainly a riverine species, commonly found in areas rich in aquatic plants. This should be kept in mind for the aquarium's decor. Oftentimes this species can initially be shy, so plenty of cover, be it plants, driftwood, or cave-type hiding places, will help them feel more comfortable. A recent study of the natural diet of *H. brachysoma* considered it to be euryphagous (eury = wide or broad; phagous = feeding or eating). This of course basically means that the fish has a varied diet and naturally eats a lot of different items, although meaty foods predominate. The meaty foods that you offer can be live, frozen, or freeze-dried and can include brine shrimp, krill, blackworms, bloodworms, etc. Make sure, though, that at least one of the regular foods is high in plant material. Although this species doesn't really prey on small fishes, such tankmates must be considered at risk, but as long as they can't be easily swallowed they should be fine.

H. nigricollaris

This is a smaller species of *Horabagrus,* but there's some conflicting literature regarding the largest size that's reached. Indian ichthyologist K. C. Jayaram lists the species at about 7 inches (18 cm) SL, but FishBase.org uses slightly over 10½ inches (27 cm) TL. The largest size that I've seen listed is on Planet Catfish—12 inches (30 cm) SL. I haven't yet seen any specimens approaching these sizes, but I'm currently raising up a group of 3 inchers (8 cm) and will see where they go from there.

This species is generally similar to *H. brachysoma* but has a lesser body depth, giving it a more elongate appearance. The body coloration also differs—it's more of a medium purplish gray/brown. Another distinguishing feature, in fact the one that gives the fish its specific epithet and its common name of black-collared catfish, is the black collar-like marking that wraps across the body behind the head region. This collar doesn't encircle the fish, but does reach almost to the pectoral fins. Behind the black collar is a whitish to gold band that goes up to the base of the dorsal fin. The caudal fin also develops a nice yellow to reddish coloration.

This species is thus far known from only one river basin in Kerala, India, and it's usually found in streams possessing a good current. So some additional water movement in the tank would be beneficial. *H. nigricollaris* is undemanding as an aquarium species. It likes to have hiding places, but I've found individual black-collared cats to rapidly leave their refuges when food is offered, even under well-lighted conditions. As with the sun cat, the species seems catholic in its food preferences and is not fussy at feeding time.

Loricariidae

The heavily armored loricariids (often generally called plecos even though not all of them bear a great resemblance to fishes of the genus *Plecostomus,* from which the "pleco" name derived) are currently very definitely among the most popular aquarium catfishes. This is the largest catfish family and consists of about 750 species in almost 100 genera. Put in another way, loricariids comprise almost 25 percent of all described catfishes. In addition to this are the numerous L-number loricariids from which many new species, and no doubt new genera, will be eventually described.

Some of the most popular and recognizable catfishes are the plecos, but this catch-all name covers numerous species (and even genera). Here is a small sample: (top left to bottom) *Acanthicus adonis*, *Baryancistrus* sp., *Hypostomus* sp., *Leporacanthicus heterodon*, *Panaque nigrolineatus*, and *Panaqolus maccus*.

L-Numbers

In the late 1980s, the German aquarium magazine *DATZ* devised a system aimed at providing a way that the numerous new and unidentified loricariids coming into the hobby could be coded. By doing this, aquarists and scientists would have a common language with which to discuss these catfishes. This system was done via publishing a photograph of a fish and then assigning it a number (called L-Number because the fishes shown belonged to the family Loricariidae). This successful system continues today, more than 20 years later, and there have been well over 400 such numbers issued.

The status of many L-Number catfishes is still unresolved. While many of them will have a genus name attached, their species status still remains a question. Certain L-Numbers have subsequently been found to be previously described species, and this information has been incorporated into the literature. Others have been described as new species, and often the L-Number will follow them along. L-46 was described as *Hypancistrus zebra*, but the number is still used today, often as an adjunct to the name.

Loricariids in Aquaria

Once wild-caught loricariids recover from their long journey to your tank, they tend to make excellent aquarium inhabitants. If you take advantage of the slowly but steadily increasing variety of tank-raised loricariids, the transition to your tanks will be even smoother. But to be sure, don't skip the watchful quarantine period even with such catfishes.

Diet

In the past the overall general assumption was that loricariids were predominately algae eaters. While there are many species that do in fact graze and feed heavily on algae, the situation is more complex than it might initially seem. The algaal covering on which many loricariids graze is much more than just algae. It's a biological cover (called periphyton or aufwuchs) that consists of, among other things, attached algae, fungi, diatoms, bacteria, and detritus. This cover usually supports a rich fauna of insects, crustaceans, and other invertebrates. The loricariids that graze on it take in a much richer source of nutrition than would be provided by algae alone. The intake of the various nonplant foods can vary greatly and depends in part on what's locally available. It can also vary depending on the season. But often the loricariid diet will consist of

10 to 15 percent meaty items. Creating a similar diet for such grazing species is not a problem—the use of a wide variety of commercial foods rich in both vegetal and animal material goes a long way towards these ends. But I believe that providing living algae and what else might be growing along with it for the catfishes to graze on is a good goal to pursue. Additionally, the feeding of some meaty foods such as bloodworms, daphnia, etc., will help to complement the nutritional profile. Observe your loricariids as you're feeding them. See what they like and what they don't like and adjust your feeding from there. Don't give up just because they may not eat something on one or two occasions, but if their disdain for what you offer continues, look for a new food item to offer. Then spread the word so that other aquarists can benefit from your observations.

Farlowella sp. (top). This twig catfish prefers strong water currents and should be kept in a small group.
Sturisoma aureum (bottom). This species is primarily herbivorous but will accept small invertebrates.

Mochokidae

This African family contains some of the most popular aquarium catfishes. Mochokidae is a fairly large family and is currently composed of 11 genera and approximately 200 species.

The overall representation of the entire family in the hobby is pretty good. I don't know whether any *Acanthocleithron* have ever been imported, but representatives of the other genera may be seen in numbers ranging from few to numerous. The greatest amount of popularity and representation within this family is based on the genus *Synodontis*, which are commonly called upside down catfishes or squeakers. The first common name is based on the swimming habits of many, but not all, of the species. The latter name is based on the sometimes rather noisy sounds that they can make by the rotating the pectoral spines in their bony sockets. These sounds can be heard both in and out of the tank. While it's not possible to go deeply into this family, I would like to start off with some brief discussion of a few genera and then narrow in somewhat on the *Synodontis* species and their closer relatives.

A Few Mochokids

A first group consists of the genera *Atopochilus, Atopodontus, Chiloglanis,* and *Euchilichthys*. These are interesting and at least superficially similar catfishes. *Atopochilus* and *Euchilichthys,* which possess flattened and elongate bodies, bear an ecological similarity in some ways to a number of loricariids. Their diet is predominately algae- and detritus-based, but they also eat some of the small invertebrates that live among the algae. As aquarium fishes they are not too fussy when it comes to feeding. You can even offer them live algae. (See Chapter 2.) These two genera can

Euchilichthys royauxi. This catfish needs good aeration and frequent water changes to thrive.

be distinguished from *Chiloglanis* in that their teeth along the width of their lower jaw are in a long line. Most of the species in these two genera are small to moderate in size, but at least one species can reach almost 16 inches (41 cm) SL.

Chiloglanis, which are widespread throughout a large part of Africa, are smaller catfishes—the maximum size of some species is around 4 inches (10 cm) SL. Although *Chiloglanis* do eat some algae, all available evidence shows them to feed predominately on insect larvae and other benthic invertebrates. Regular feedings with meatier foods can supplement the more standard fare of commercial foods, which they generally take to with no major problems once they are settled into a tank. *Chiloglanis* can be easily distinguished from *Atopochilus* and *Euchilichthys* in that the teeth in their lower jaw form into a small bunched group in the middle of the jaw. This fits well with the invertebrate-picker natural style of feeding.

The four mentioned genera in this group are typically found in flowing water, so their oxygen requirements in captivity are increased, and their tolerance for built-up waste is rather low. Consequently, as a group they don't hold up as well as many other catfishes do in the collecting, holding, and shipping processes, but those that I've worked with that did make it through this regimen adapted well to aquarium life. Be sure to provide these catfishes with good, or extra, aeration and a current in their tank. It's also good practice to do larger and more frequent water changes than those usually done for other members of the family.

Synodontis

The genus *Synodontis* is very close to the top of my personal favorites list. It was this group that initially caught my fancy when I mainly kept cichlids. *Synodontis* slowly replaced the cichlids, and before I knew it I was a confirmed catfish keeper—and I've never turned back.

Genera and Number of Species in the Family Mochokidae

Acanthocleithron 1 species
Atopochilus 7 species
Atopodontus 1 species
Chiloglanis 45 species
Euchilichthys 5 species
Microsynodontis 12 species
Mochokiella 1 species
Mochokus 2 species
Synodontis 128 species

Note: The monotypic genera *Brachysynodontis* (= *Synodontis batensoda*) and *Hemisynodontis* (= *Synodontis membranacea*) are herein included as species in the genus *Synodontis*.

On *Synodontis* Species Names

In the Ferraris paper the reader is presented with some different forms of the spelling of 32 *Synodontis* names. This results from using *Synodontis* as a feminine name; since the endings of the specific epithets applied to a given species are supposed to agree in grammatical gender with the gender of the generic name, and since previously the name *Synodontis* had been generally accepted as masculine, the ending of many of the specific names of *Synodontis* species now might be different from the name under which the species was originally named. The old names ended in –*us*, and the new forms end in –*a*. Thus *S. albolineatus* is now *S. albolineata*, *S. angelicus* is *S. angelica*, etc.

This genus has a wide distribution throughout sub-Sahara Africa but is absent in the very southern part of the continent. Even in the north where rivers go through the desert (e.g., the Nile) at least some *Synodontis* may be found. As this is being written there are 128 described species, so as you would expect there's quite a bit of size variation. There are some smaller species that are only a few inches long, while others can reach and exceed 2 feet (60 cm). Most of the species tend towards the lower-middle end of the scale, and there are a wide variety of aquarium species that fall into the nice size class of about 4 to 12 inches (10 to 30 cm). Although there are many variations in their general body form, the great majority of species are fairly similar in overall body shape. There are some exceptions to this, especially in some of the fast-water species like *S. brichardi,* which tend to have a more elongate and flattened body. The colors and patterns that exist in the genus are also quite varied, and this is one of the things that enhance their popularity.

As aquarium catfishes, *Synodontis* present no special problems. Like all other catfishes they appreciate good water quality, so a regimen of regular water changes, coupled with good mechanical and biological filtration, should be maintained. As regards pH values the fishes accept a wide range. The temperature for *Synodontis* can range from 72° to 78°F (22° to 26°C). The *Synodontis* tank(s) should have some open space, as these catfishes generally like to swim around. However, hiding places should also be provided.

Feeding *Synodontis* is the definition of "easy." I can't recall anything from the standard catfish menu that a happy and healthy fish wouldn't eat. In addition to the standard commercial foods, be sure and include a good amount of meaty foods in any format. Bloodworms are a particular favorite of any *Synodontis* catfish.

Synodontis species come into the hobby from three main geographical areas: West Africa, the Congo, and the great lakes of eastern Africa. Below is a short look at some of the available species.

Congo: The Congo (Zaire) River basin provides some of the nicest *Synodontis* species. As with Nigeria, shipments of these and other fishes are currently not up to historical standards, but there have been some improvements as of late. This will hopefully at least stay steady and possibly increase in the near future.

S. alberti: This is an attractive but not overly colorful species. The base coloration is silvery brown, often with a nice purplish cast (especially in juveniles), and there are larger dark spots of varying size on the body. What makes this an interesting species is the combination of large eyes, a long dorsal fin, and very long maxillary barbels. The barbels on this fish are the longest in the genus and are proportionally longer in young fish. *S. alberti* is a peaceful species that can reach a little less than 9 inches (23 cm) SL. Due to their mild manners and the long barbels it's best to keep *S. alberti* with peaceful, non-nipping fishes.

S. angelica: For many years this fish was considered the tops in *Synodontis* species. Though dethroned by *S. granulosa,* it's still a popular and desirable species. The "typical" *S. angelica* is a dark black fish with white spots scattered all over the head and body. These spots can vary and sometimes present a pattern of numerous small spots or less numerous larger spots. On occasion narrow winding bands of the same color as the spots can also be seen. There are a number of variations with

Typical *Synodontis* Features

- The body is naked (no plating, etc.) and thick-skinned.
- The head, and the nape up to the dorsal spine, are enclosed in a bony armor.
- The bony dorsal spine and pectoral spines are well developed. Remember this when netting and handling these catfishes.
- They have three pairs of barbels: the maxillary pair (upper lip) and two mandibular pairs (chin barbels). The chin barbels are always branched in varying degrees, depending on the species involved. The maxillary pair is usually not branched, but there are a few species that do show branching of the maxillaries.

These features also generally fit for the related monotypic genus *Mochokiella* (*M. paynei* is the species). The care of this species is exactly as with a typical *Synodontis.*

S. angelica. This species tends to be territorial about its hiding spot.

the spot coloration; they may range from light bluish to yellow. *S. angelica* isn't a nasty species, but individuals can be territorial and will effectively protect a hiding place that they want to call home. A size of a little less than 10 inches (25 cm) SL is reached, and these larger individuals usually appear to be females.

S. brichardi: This elongated species is a very attractive *Synodontis* with a fairly limited distribution. It has evolved to live in rapids and will do much better if provided with a good current in its tank. Good biological filtration and frequent larger-than-usual water changes are also helpful. *S. brichardi* is a social species and does nicely in groups. There has been some reproductive activity reported (without the laying of eggs), which makes this a potentially very interesting species to work with. Females of this species can reach up to at least 8 inches (20 cm) TL.

S. congica: This peaceful silvery large-eyed species is ideal for a mild-mannered tank. On the side of the body are a varying number of round black spots. Sometimes these are smaller and in groups when seen around the caudal peduncle. Although reported to reach up to 8 inches (20 cm) TL, most *S. congica* are somewhat smaller.

S. contracta: One of my favorites! This small species (4 inches [10 cm] TL) looks like a somewhat boxier and larger-eyed version of *S. nigriventris*. *S. contracta* is quite social and ideally should be kept in groups. Based on the various good factors of this species it would seem to have great potential for a breeding attempt project.

S. decora: Without question this is one of the most magnificent Congo *Synodontis*. The

On *Synodontis* Hybrids

I must comment on the hybrid *Synodontis* that have been coming into the hobby. Most of these fishes originate in eastern Europe and are, in my opinion, not a positive development for the hobby. Some of them come with valid scientific names attached—*S. granulosa* and *S. ornatipinnis* come immediately to mind. Sometimes the hybrids do resemble the real species, but there are usually some subtle differences. The prices asked for these fishes are high, befitting the generally uncommon and expensive status of the two species mentioned. In other cases they come with common names, or designations, attached to them.

base coloration is whitish, often with a pinkish cast, and there's a patterning of black markings on the body. The distinguishing feature of note is the long black trailer that develops on the dorsal fin. Although the length may vary, in some adults it will reach back to, or past, the caudal fin. Based on this trailer, it's best to avoid nippy tankmates. *S. decora* can eventually reach around 13 inches (33 cm) TL. A small group of this species growing up in a 6-foot-long (2-m-long) tank is a vision to behold!

S. flavitaeniata: This is as beautiful a catfish as you're likely to find anywhere. Its distinctive color pattern has led to the common name pajamas syno in the UK. This is a mild-mannered species that reaches a little less than 8 inches (20 cm) TL.

S. nigriventris: This is the classic upside-down catfish. Although it's not overly colorful,

S. decora. This is one of the larger *Synodontis*, reaching a length near 13 inches (33 cm).

its upside-down aquatic ballet is a pleasure to watch. This is a peaceful and smaller (4 inches [10 cm] TL) schooling species and should be maintained in groups (a minimum of four). When obtaining this catfish, beware of some of the spotted West African species that might also be sold as U-D cats. Also, I've seen an Asian bagrid (*Mystus leucophasis*) being sold as *S. nigriventris,* a nice catfish but a world away when it comes to behavior and sociability.

S. notata: If you're looking for a larger *Synodontis* species that can give as well as it takes, this species could be for you. *S. notata* has a gray body and displays one or many round black spots on its sides. Although it isn't a nasty species, it can take care of itself. Since it will reach around 10½ inches (27 cm) TL, it can be a good choice for a community situation with larger and possibly somewhat rowdy fishes.

S. ornatipinnis: To come upon one of these rare cats is always a special event. Though uncommonly imported, *S. ornatipinnis* is well worth getting should you find one or more. Youngsters resemble *S. brichardi* with wider than normal darker bands. As they grow this pattern slowly breaks up (from front to back) into a series of irregular large spots. *S. ornatipinnis* reaches a maximum length of 10 inches (25 cm) TL.

S. flavitaeniata (top), a fairly peaceful species. *S. nigriventris* (top center). Although other fishes may be sold under the same name, this is the fish usually called the upside-down catfish. *S. notata* (bottom center). This syno is a good choice for a community tank of large, boisterous fish. *S. ornatipinnis* (bottom). Young specimens of this infrequently seen mochokid could be confused with *S. brichardi*. This photo shows the adult pattern.

S. schoutedeni: It can be difficult to find a *Synodontis* species that is prettier and more personable than this one. It is, without question, quite beautiful and falls within a nice adult size range—a little less than 7 inches (18 cm) TL. This is definitely a species that you might wish to set up a dedicated tank for. There have been successful captive spawnings, so it's ideal for additional breeding projects.

S. soloni. This species adjusts well to aquarium life, and does enjoy a bit of extra water current.

Additional Synodontis: Other *Synodontis* species that may be encountered in Congo shipments include: *S. acanthomias, S. aterrima, S. camelopardalis, S. caudalis, S. depauwi, S. greshoffi, S. longirostris, S. nummifer, S. pleurops, S. pulcher, S. robertsi,* and *S. soloni.* The potential for other known and unknown species is also there. So keep your eyes open when any Congo shipments are around. You never know what might show up.

Great Lakes: The great lakes of east Africa are well known for their cichlids, but there are also some very interesting *Synodontis* species that dwell therein.

Lake Malawi: There is nominally one species (*S. njassae*) available from this lake. It's a silvery/coppery species with numerous small black spots on the body. While this fish is more elongate and matches nicely with the original description, a look-alike species may possibly be seen from time to time. It has a higher body and a pattern of larger but fewer spots. Whether this turns out to be an undescribed species, as has been suggested, remains to be seen.

Lake Tanganyika: There was recently a revision of the *Synodontis* species from this lake, and a total of ten endemic species were recognized. There's also one non-endemic to be found in the lake (*S. nigromaculata*).

S. grandiops: In most ways this species is like *S. multipunctata* with almost identical color patterns. However, there are some distinguishing differences:

• *S. grandiops* (the name means large eye) has, in relation to the head size, a much larger eye. The overall appearance of this makes the snout appear shorter.

- The soft ray count on the pectoral fin differs. With *S. multipunctata* there are eight rays, but in *S. grandiops* there are only seven. This can be viewed directly by holding the fish up to the tank's glass, or perhaps better by getting close-up digital photos to work with.
- The top edge of the triangular humeral process is concave in *S. multipunctata* while in *S. grandiops* it's convex.
- There is a difference in the maximal sizes noted between the two species, but this is likely not to be of help, considering the usual size of the fish that are imported. The maximal size of *S. grandiops* is listed at a little under 6 inches (15 cm) TL, while *S. multipunctata* reaches a little over 11 inches (28 cm) TL. I—and no one I know—have ever seen one close to this large size.

The importance of separating these two catfishes among wild stock is that they are, of course, different species. As this is being written I have been unable to find any definite spawning reports for *S. grandiops*. However, some illustrated Internet material on spawning *S. multipunctata* would appear to actually involve *S. grandiops*. It would be an important contribution to the hobby to breed this species and be able to confirm or deny whether it's also a cuckoo-style spawner (more on this in a moment).

S. granulosa: This is the current top-shelf species of the genus. The purple-gray body framed with black and white fins makes for a beautifully dramatic appearance. But make no mistake—you will pay a hefty sum to have one of these cats swimming in your

S. granulosa. This species can be territorial about its caves. Have at least one hiding place for each individual.

tanks. There are reports from the UK that the true species has been bred in aquaria, but details are so far unavailable. It is reported to grow to 10½ inches (27 cm).

S. lucipinnis: This is one of the newer (2006) *Synodontis* species. It's elongate, kind of tube-shaped, and

Synodontis grandiops is quite similar to *S. multipunctata*, but the larger eye and shorter snout are helpful diagnostic characters.

is similar to *S. petricola*, with a maximum size of 3 inches (8 cm). It appears that *S. lucipinnis* is, at least in part, the species involved in the so-called *S. "dwarf petricola"* that are seen in the hobby. I say in part in that there isn't necessarily good consistency in the use of many common names. This situation is slowly being straightened out, and hopefully more information will be forthcoming in the near future. But be aware of the situation.

S. multipunctata: This is one of the long-time favorites among the Tanganyikan *Synodontis*. Not only is it attractive, but it's also the most commonly spawned of all the *Synodontis* species. It's well documented in nature and captivity that this species is a cuckoo-style spawner that lays its eggs among those of spawning mouthbrooding cichlids while eating some of the cichlid eggs along the way. The catfish eggs are then picked up, along with its own diminished lot of eggs, by the cichlid for brooding. The catfish eggs hatch rather quickly, and the fry then feast on the cichlid's eggs that are being brooded as their first food. *S. multipunctata* adapts well to various situations, and the great majority of aquarium cuckoo-style spawnings take place with Lake Malawi cichlids.

In 2006, with the description of *S. grandiops*, the situation with *S. multipunctata* became a bit more interesting. *S. grandiops* strongly resembles *S. multipunctata,* and both species have been imported into the hobby, which may cause some confusion and misidentification among dealers and hobbyists.

Lake Victoria: S. *victoriae* (14½ inches [37 cm] is from this lake and some of its streams and satellite lakes. Currently there is minimal commercial collecting in this area, so *S. victoriae* is rarely seen. *S. afrofischeri* (8 inches [21 cm]), although not bound to the lake and its immediate environs, has appeared in shipments from the lake.

West Africa: Historically, Nigeria has shipped in the largest quantities of West African *Synodontis*. Such shipments consisted of more than a few, usually spotted, species typically sold as U-D cats. Mixed in among these one could usually find interesting by-catch species. Certain recognizable species may now be separated out and sold under their species name (e.g., *S. clarias*), usually at a premium. As of late, though, the political situation in Nigeria has led to an overall cutback in both the number and variety of *Synodontis* shipped. Hopefully in the future this will change.

S. clarias: This is a distinctively colored species. The body is gray to gray-brown, often with scattered small dark spots present. The highlight of this species is its noticeably red caudal fin, which also tends to show a patterning of scattered dark spots. *S. clarias* is one of the few species that shows branching on the maxillary barbels. This species can reach almost 13 inches (33 cm) SL.

S. euptera: Although not overly colorful (winding bands in juveniles, gray body with black spots in adults), this species has become a hobby favorite due to the form of its dorsal fin. As the fish grows the first ray becomes prolonged and the rest of the rays follow suit, although not quite as long. This gives the fin a feathery appearance, the inspiration for the common name feather-fin catfish. As with many other *Synodontis*, this is a long-lived fish (more than 25 years) that can eventually

S. euptera. There are records for this species of individuals living in the aquarium for more than 25 years.

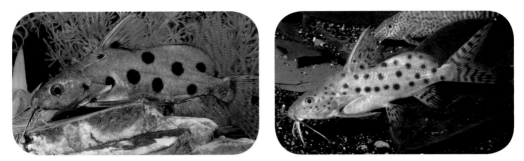

S. ocellifer. The juveniles (left) have fewer and darker spots than the adults (right).

reach about 10½ inches (27 cm) SL. This species has been commercially bred by some fish farms.

S. ocellifer: This is an attractive species with a grayish base color (often with a yellow cast) and large round black spots on the body. As the fish grows, some of these spots will clear in the center, forming an ocelli-type appearance. The caudal fin has a pattern of banding on both lobes. Based on wild-caught fish, this species can reach around 19 inches (48 cm) SL, although I have personally never seen any aquarium individuals reaching anywhere near this. A more common aquarium range is about 8 to 9 inches (20 to 23 cm) SL. This species has been commercially bred, and a few years ago at least one Florida fish farm was providing juveniles to the hobby.

Pimelodidae

This South American family (Heptapteridae and Pseudopimelodidae used to be included in the Pimelodidae), which is composed of around 100 described species divided among 29 genera, contains some of the largest and most popular of the neotropical food catfishes. In the included sidebar are the names of 20 genera in this family and the maximal sizes that both their smallest and largest species are known to attain. A number of the genera are monotypic, in which case the size is based on the one included species. Sometimes a range is provided. The lower end number with these genera may be valid or could just represent a lack of study material. In any case, with the difficulty of identifying some of these fishes, especially in their juvenile forms, the upper end range given is a worst case scenario. In my opinion, the catfishes in the sidebar should not be kept in home aquaria. It's not only the size that's taken into account; the general behavior of these catfishes is also considered. Besides getting very large, most of them are fast-moving predators. The confines of even the largest home aquarium don't agree with this lifestyle. And even if they learn a lesson from smashing into the aquarium glass once too often, why keep a large and magnificent catfish that just lies there, barely able to turn around?

Please try to not be drawn into getting any of these giants in their juvenile form. Research the fishes and think doubly hard about what you're going to do when they start to grow. The potential problems are large for both aquarist and catfish.

This family also contains a number of genera in which the size or behavioral characteristics potentially speak well for them as aquarium catfishes. Unfortunately, comparatively few of these cats are imported into the hobby. The one genus that does have some potential for aquarium use is *Pimelodus*, but admittedly there are even some good-sized catfishes (12 to 15 inches [30 to 38 cm] SL) in this large genus (around 30 species). The most commonly seen species is *P. pictus,* which is often seen under the trade name *P.* *"angelicus."* Imported from Colombia and Peru, this catfish is a smaller

Say No to Pangasiidae

This Asian family of large to very large catfishes currently contains four genera and 28 species. One species has a long aquarium history: the iridescent shark *Pangasianodon hypophthalmus,* which is most often marketed to newer aquarists because of the use of the name "shark." This fish is seen in both normal (gray/silver) and albino color forms and is typically 2 to 4 inches (5 to 10 cm) when encountered in pet stores. Usually they're sold with no mention that the adult size is around 4½ feet (1.3 m) and that they become hyper as they grow. This behavioral characteristic usually ends up sending them in fast flight into the aquarium glass again and again. It's uncommon to see larger specimens (say even 6 to 8 inches [15 to 20 cm]) that don't show some permanent damage to their

nasal area. Individuals are even more nervous when not kept in a school of at least six. This isn't a good aquarium catfish, and it should be completely avoided.

Even more insane is the occasional importation of small individuals of *Pangasius sanitwongsei,* a species known to reach 9 feet (2.7 m) and over 650 pounds (295 kg)!

Large Pimelodids

Aguarunichthys 12½ to 16½ inches (32 to 42 cm) SL
Brachyplatystoma 2 to 11½ feet (60 cm to 3.5 m) TL
Calophysus 15½ inches (39 cm) TL
Hemisorubim 21 inches (53 cm) SL
Hypophthalmus 22 inches (56 cm) TL
Leiarius 24 inches (61 cm) TL
Luciopimelodus 37 inches (94 cm) SL
Megalonema 12 inches (30 cm) TL
Perrunichthys 24 inches (61 cm) TL
Phractocephalus 50 inches (1.3 m) TL

Pimelodina 14 inches (36 cm) TL
Pinirampus 47 inches (1.2 m) TL
Platynematichthys 32 inches (81 cm) SL
Platysilurus 8 to 27 inches (20 to 69 cm) SL
Platystomatichthys 15½ inches (39 cm) TL
Pseudoplatystoma 54 inches (1.4 m) SL
Sorubim 10 to 31½ inches (25 to 80 cm) SL
Sorubimichthys 60 inches (1.5 m) SL
Steindachneridion 16 to 22 inches (41 to 56 cm) SL
Zungaro 52 inches (1.3 m) SL

species, reaching a maximum length of slightly under 5 inches (13 cm) SL. The base color is a silvery white. The body is covered with a random pattern of black spots; these are also seen on the fins. The spots on the fins form patterns of a sort, especially on the dorsal and caudal fins. Differences in the spotted patterns of different populations can be noted. These differences can include the size and number of the spots. The maxillary barbels on this species are noticeably long and will reach back to at least the base of the caudal fin. The barbels are almost constantly moving around, helping the fish to find tidbits of food. As with many other pimelodids, the dorsal and pectoral fins are armed with formidable, if smaller, spines. Feeding won't be a problem with this catfish. In the wild it's a typical carnivore and eats small fishes as well as a wide variety of insects and aquatic invertebrates. This is definitely worth keeping in mind—smaller fishes in the same tank would definitely be at risk with this species.

P. pictus is a schooling species, so be sure to purchase at least three or more so that you can observe their group dynamics, which can really be quite pretty to watch. This might also offer up some experiences with spawning this catfish. I'm not aware of any spawning reports, so there's your challenge.

One last "Pimelodus" worthy of discussion is the catfish called the four-line pim in the trade. I put Pimelodus in quotes here in that over a period of time a number of species may be seen under the same common name. You will see some with a light horizontal lined pattern (these may be P. albofasciatus or other similar species), but you may also observe fish with a pattern of large spots on the body. Others may be seen that exhibit

Luciopimelodus pati. Like many others among the pimelodids, this species is too large and active for the home aquarium.

little or no pattern. Many of them can be expected to reach an eventual adult size of 6 to 9 inches (15 to 23 cm) SL, so keep this in mind in regard to their housing. As with *P. pictus,* these various species will eat smaller fishes. These catfishes display group dynamics, so ideally you should get two or three and let them grow up together.

Pseudopimelodidae

This is a small South American family (some authorities still maintain that it belongs to the family Pimelodidae) consisting of 29 species divided among five genera. Many are quite colorful and present a pattern of dark bands or blotches on a yellow to orange base color. The smaller species of the genus *Microglanis* exhibiting this color pattern are popular as aquarium catfishes and are usually sold as bumblebee cats. Some of the larger species of the genus *Pseudopimelodus*

Pimelodus pictus. This species schools, so keep a small group of them in the aquarium.

Cephalosilurus fowleri. The wide mouth and small eyes are typical for the family.

also exhibit a similar pattern; they too have a following among aquarists liking medium-sized (up to almost 10 inches [25 cm] SL) predatory catfishes. I have seen them sometimes sold as giant bumblebee cats. One feature that all pseudopimelodids share is a noticeably wide mouth. They also have comparatively small eyes.

All of these catfishes that I've maintained make for good aquarium fishes. But you should realize that they're all predatory to varying degrees. Even the smaller *Microglanis* species, such as *M. iheringi* (the common South American bumblebee cat of the hobby), which feed predominately on insects and other invertebrates in the wild, may not be able to resist any small fishes that might be kept in the same tank. And "small" is a relative word. The shape of the tankmates is also important. Longer and thinner tankmates may be potentially partially swallowed and then slowly digested over a period of days. Larger *Batrochoglanis* and *Pseudopimelodus* have an eating capacity that can be quite amazing, so equally large, or even larger, tankmates must be chosen. But even this at times may not be a sure thing.

From time to time you may also see *Cephalosilurus* species. These are larger (some grow to over 15 inches [38 cm] SL) highly predatory species that are sometimes sold under the name jelly cats. The eating capacity of these catfishes is nothing short of amazing, so great care must be taken in choosing tankmates. Don't underestimate these cats!

Microglanis at a Glance

The genus *Microglanis* contains 14 species, and as noted *M. iheringi* is the most commonly seen species. But even with shipments of that species, slightly different-looking specimens may be seen from time to time. These might just be variations, but there's also the chance that some different species may be mixed in with the *M. iheringi*. The trained eye can often come up with some potentially different and interesting catfishes.

M. iheringi, which reaches a maximal size of only 2¼ inches (6 cm) SL, is an ideal little aquarium catfish (just remember the caveat regarding small tankmates). Provide them with tropical temperatures, a moderate pH (6.5 to 7.2), and good-quality water and they will thrive. They do well in small groups and are gregarious feeders on just about anything you care to feed them. Like most other bottom-hugging catfishes they appreciate hiding places. In Peru I found them to be quite common among leaf litter in one small and shallow stream. They have been spawned in aquaria on a number of occasions; duplicating this achievement would be something to easily spark your interest.

Schilbeidae

The schilbeid catfishes have representation in Africa and Asia. There are indications that the two geographical groups may not be closely related, and if this proves to be the case the Asian members would end up being placed into a separate family. As it stands now there are a total of 58 species in 12 genera. This differs slightly from the figures in Ferraris, the difference being based on two genera (*Platytropius, Pseudeutropius*) with four species that have been included herein in the family Horabagridae.

All schilbeids are mid-water swimming fishes and all tend towards being laterally compressed. Usually they have a dorsal and adipose fin, but either or both of these fins may be absent. The pectoral fins in all species are armed with a strong spine. The anal fin is long and the caudal fin is forked. The number of usually long barbels can vary; two or four pairs may be present. The eyes are usually large.

A number of these catfishes are imported into the hobby. Arguably the most commonly seen is the West African *Schilbe intermedius* (seen in older aquarium literature as *S. mystus*), which is sold under the name grass cutter cat. While these catfish are attractive at the smaller sizes at which they're are imported (about 3 inches [8 cm] SL), their colors mute as they grow. And grow they do, reaching a maximum size of around 2 feet (60 cm) TL. Nice when young, but grown up they don't make for a good aquarium species.

The best aquarium fishes in this family are the ones that are commonly called African glass catfishes. There are two genera and five species involved in this group—*Parailia congica* and *Parailia pellucida,* and *Pareutropius buffei, Pareutropius debauwi,*

Microglanis iheringi. This tiny catfish has spawned under aquarium conditions.

and *Pareutropius mandevillei*. None of these catfishes gets very large. They can range from about 3½ to 6 inches (9 to 15 cm) TL, with *P. mandevillei* coming in smaller at about 2½ inches (6 cm) TL. Shipments and numbers of these species can vary greatly, but one feature they share is that all of them are as likely as not to also be marketed as debauwi cats. When you do see a tank of these fishes , examine them closely. Sometimes shipments, or parts thereof, may be mixed, so you might be able to come up with more than one species.

The care of these cats is similar, and they all should be provided with ample swimming space. Ideally, plants (whether real or artificial) can be situated along the sides and the back of the tank, creating a swimming "theater" in the center. All of the mentioned species are schooling catfishes and should be kept in groups (a minimum of four, though six to eight would even be better). These are very peaceful catfishes and are ideal for a mild-mannered community tank. They aren't fussy as regards foods, but a variety of small meaty foods should be considered mandatory.

Siluridae

For all of the variety that exists within this Euro-Asian family (12 genera containing about 95 species, two of them in Europe), there are relatively few reasonable aquarium species. For the most part the catfishes in this family are large, predatory, and fast-moving mid-water species. Some, such as *Wallago* and *Belodontichthys* for example, just don't belong in aquaria. They and other related fast-moving catfishes are not able to live comfortably in a glass box.

Meet *Schilbe marmoratus*

Schilbe marmoratus is a very attractive species with a pleasing dark mottled pattern on a tan to light brown body. It is around 9 inches (23 cm) SL. They will eat just about anything and aren't generally a problem species.

Silurids, especially the mid-water forms, tend to have a laterally compressed body. Others, such as *Silurus*, and some smaller but similar species, tend to be more elongate and rounded in body form. These latter species are generally more associated with the bottom, but they do rise into the water column to feed. Silurids have a small dorsal fin that doesn't have a spine, but in some cases the dorsal fin may be altogether absent. The pectoral fins have spines, so take care with these. The ventral fins are usually small and may be absent in some species. All members of this family also lack an adipose fin.

There are also some ideal aquarium species residing in this family, including the very popular Asian glass catfish. Because this fish is a staple in the general hobby, it is often unappreciated by some catfish fans. It's a good species for a peaceful community tank, but also one worthy of more attention from the catfish fancier. The genus *Kryptopterus*, to which the glass catfish belongs, is widespread in Asia, Malaysia, and Indonesia, and a number of species enter the hobby from time to time. In all there are 18 described species. The most commonly seen is *K. minor*. This catfish has apparently been in the hobby for over 70 years, mostly under the incorrect name *K. bicirrhis,* which is actually a larger species. But historical hobby photos and drawings do also seem to indicate that at least a couple of species (or even more) have apparently been imported under this name over the years.

Parailia pellucida, an African glass catfish, needs to be kept in a school (at least four to five individuals) and should be provided with ample open water space for swimming.

K. minor is a small (about 3 inches [8 cm] SL), peaceful species that should be kept in groups. Other fishes that are kept with them should be peaceful in nature. This is a mid-to-upper water fish; ample swimming room should be provided. This species also enjoys some milder current to swim in, and accommodations should be made for this. There should ideally be plants (real are best, but artificial will work) to provide hiding and security places. Tall rooted plants in a forest formation are perfect for the purpose. Some floating plants will also help to make them feel secure. A good cover of something like duckweed will be excellent.

Kryptopterus minor. This species lives in schools and does best when housed with some tall plants to hide among.

Feeding *K. minor* is not a problem; it will take a variety of prepared and meaty foods—emphasis on the latter. This species, especially in a group, is enjoyable to watch when they are feeding. Their agility is quite fascinating. Water conditions aren't critical, but the fish will look a little better and act a little happier in slightly acid water. Temperatures are as with standard tropical values.

There is one thing to avoid with this species: the dye-injected individuals that show up from time to time. Don't purchase these fish! The dye-injecting of all fishes, including catfishes, should be harshly discouraged.

So Many More

As was stated earlier, this chapter is just a brief introduction to the world of catfishes. There are many more available, and that's both good and bad. Some will make ideal aquarium inhabitants, while others should be avoided at all costs. Catfishes to avoid include species that are dangerous, endangered, or even illegal to own as well as those that are simply too big. But don't let that turn you off to the wonderful catfishes. If you decide to keep them, you're truly in for something special. Enjoy!

Resources

Magazine & Online Forum

Tropical Fish Hobbyist
1 TFH Plaza
3rd & Union Avenues
Neptune City, NJ 07753
E-mail: info@tfh.com
www.tfhmagazine.com

Internet Resources

TFH Magazine & Online Forum
www.tfhmagazine.com

TFH Magazine Forum
http://forums.tfhmagazine.com

Aquaria Central
www.aquariacentral.com

Aquarium Hobbyist
www.aquariumhobbyist.com

Microcosm Aquarium Explorer
www.microcosmaquariumexplorer.com

Planet Catfish
www.planetcatfish.com/

ScotCat
www.scotcat.com

Wet Web Media
www.wetwebmedia.com

Associations and Societies

Federation of American Aquarium
Societies (FAAS)
E-mail: Jbenes01@yahoo.com

www.faas.info

Books

Boruchowitz, David. *The Simple Guide to Freshwater Aquariums*. TFH Publications, Inc.

Hellweg, Michael R. *Culturing Live Foods*. TFH Publications, Inc.

Ward, Ashley. *Questions & Answers on Freshwater Aquarium Fishes*. TFH Publications, Inc.

Index

Dedication

I cordially dedicate this work to Julian (Jools) Dignall of PlanetCatfish and Allan James of ScotCat for first turning the soil on the electronic frontier of aquarium catfishes and their dedication to the continued nurturing of it.

But most of all I dedicate this to my wife Aline, who is my constant helper in doing things in my admittedly old-fashioned ways.

Acknowledgments

To do this properly I would need to list everyone in both the hobby and science communities with whom I've communicated with regarding catfishes. This would be, of course, impossible, but please know that all of you have made the catfish experience an interesting and wonderful one. But I guess that I should have a beginning and an end for this piece. For the beginning I thank Ray Horn [RIP] who first encouraged my interest in catfishes. The end of this project is also a beginning, so I shall wait and see where it takes me and to whom it introduces me.

About the author

Lee Finley has been an aquarium hobbyist/professional for over 40 years. As an integral part of this, Lee has regularly written on various aquarial topics over the past 30 years and has over 335 published articles to his credit. Among these writings are included almost 12 years of a monthly book review column and almost nine years of a monthly catfish column in Tropical Fish Hobbyist Magazine.

Lee has enjoyed the pleasures of many different fishes over the years and many of his early experiences were predominately with cichlids. From there he moved on to catfishes and this fascinating group has kept him interested and challenged for the past 28 or so years. This interest has prompted some travel, and Lee has made

four trips to South America (Brazil and Peru) to observe and catch catfishes in their natural habitat.

Lee has been involved in many other aspects of the aquarium hobby/industry. In the past he was owner/operator of an independent pet store. For the last 10 years, Lee has run a predominately mail order book business (Finley Aquatic Books) dealing in both new and used literature encompassing all aspects of the aquarium hobby and aquatic natural history.

Photo Credits

Deborah Aronds (courtesy of Shutterstock): 20

Glen S. Axelrod: 26

Al Connelly: 48

Dmitriyd (courtesy of Shutterstock): 34

Andreas Gradin (courtesy of Shutterstock): 5, 28

Hansen: 79 (left)

David D. Herlong: 109

Ray Hunziker: 36 (left)

Matt Jones (courtesy of Shutterstock): cover, 1

Gary Lange: 41

Horst Linke: 106 (top center), 119

Oliver Lucanus: 11, 17, 82, 106 (bottom), 110, 111 (right)

Aaron Norman: 66 (left), 73 (all), 78 (center left, bottom left), 80, 90, 91, 100, 115, 117, 118

John O'Malley: 88, 97 (bottom left), 105

M.P. and C. Piednoir: 75

Hans-Joachim Richter: 77 (center right), 85, and back cover (top)

Marcelo Saavedra (courtesy of Shutterstock): 92

Dr. Jurgen Schmidt: 4, 13, 15, 57 (all), 71, 78 (bottom right), 107, 114 (bottom)

I. Seidel: 54

Craig Sernotti: 36 (right)

Mark Smith: 6, 66 (right), 78 (center right), 81, 86, 89 (top), 95 (top), 97 (top left, top right, center left), 99 (bottom), 108

Edward Taylor: 60, 89 (bottom), 94

All other images from TFH archives.

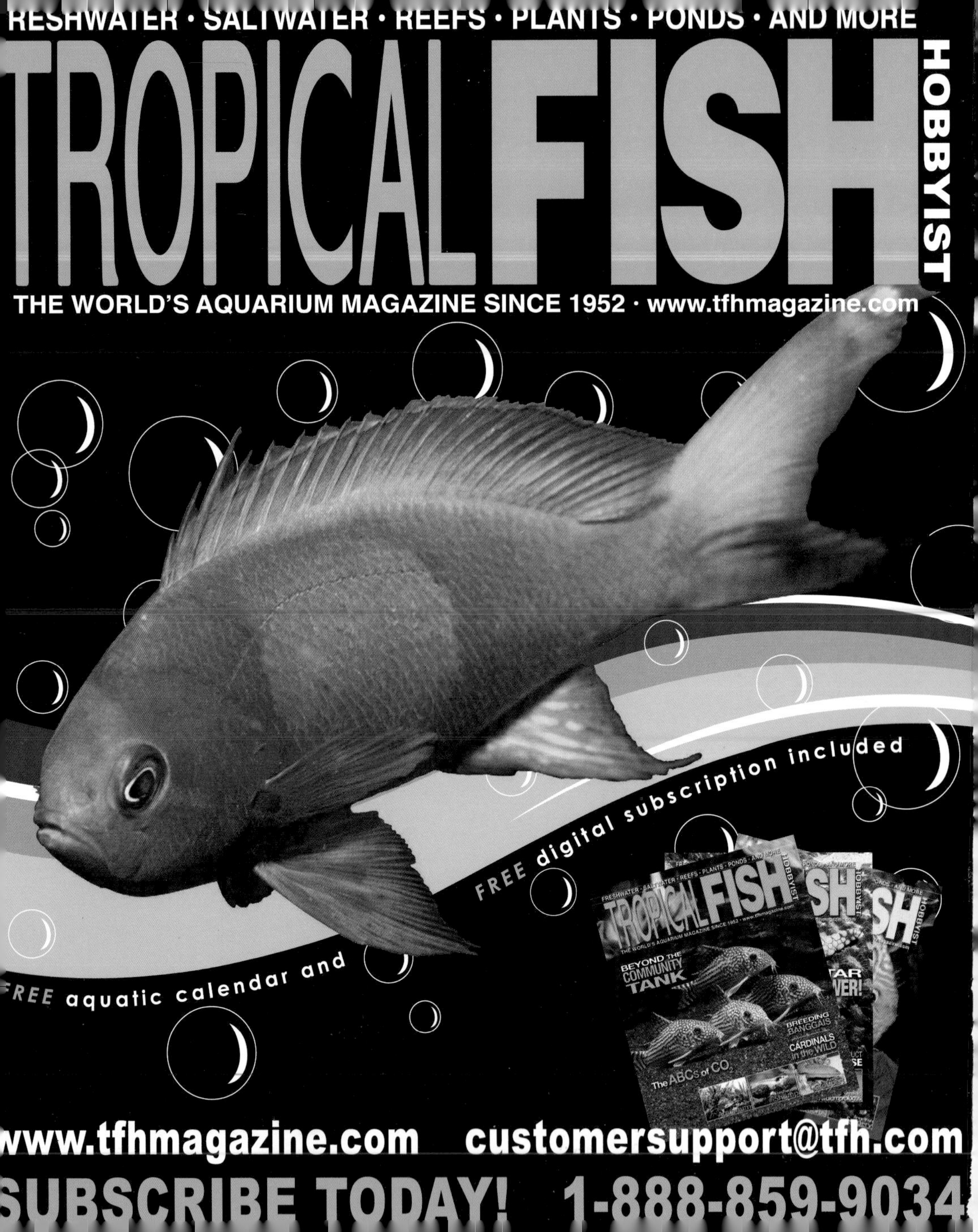

RESHWATER · SALTWATER · REEFS · PLANTS · PONDS · AND MORE
TROPICAL FISH HOBBYIST
THE WORLD'S AQUARIUM MAGAZINE SINCE 1952 · www.tfhmagazine.com
FREE aquatic calendar and FREE digital subscription included
TROPICAL FISH HOBBYIST
BEYOND THE COMMUNITY TANK
BREEDING BANGGAIS
CARDINALS in the WILD
The ABCs of CO2
www.tfhmagazine.com
customersupport@tfh.com
SUBSCRIBE TODAY! 1-888-859-9034